ENTER DRUM
AND COLOURS

Memories of National Service in the 1950's

To Julie

ENTER DRUM AND COLOURS

Memories of National Service in the 1950's

Alan Brewin

BREWIN BOOKS

First published by
Brewin Books Ltd, 56 Alcester Road,
Studley, Warwickshire B80 7LG in 2004
www.brewinbooks.com

ISBN 1 85858 241 5

A Cataloguing in Publication Record
for this title is available from the British Library.

Typeset in Caslon
Printed in Great Britain by
Warwick Printing Company Limited.

CONTENTS

ACKNOWLEDGEMENTS

I would like to thank the many people who have helped me bring this book to publication. First and foremost, thanks go to my wife Julie who has had to tolerate tables in various parts of the house covered with maps, manuscripts, photographs and old documents for weeks on end. My warmest thanks also go to Alistair who is my son and also the company's art editor. He is responsible for the overall design, typeface, style, illustrations and general production of the book. Publication is also due in no small part to encouragement received from my daughters Amanda and Stephanie. Thanks go, of course, to Val Homer, my secretary for many years for deciphering my manuscript and converting it to computer disk. Paul Yates too of Warwick Printing has given me his usual courteous and efficient help.

The Imperial War Museum has been extremely helpful in filling one or two gaps in the illustrations needed, although most of the photographs in the book were taken and processed by myself or taken using my camera. Other Associations proffering help with names, addresses or dates include the RAEC Association, The Old Edwardians Association and The National Army Museum. I would like especially to thank Lt. Colonel Aubrey Chalmers, County President of The Royal British Legion, Warwickshire, for his support and for kindly supplying a Foreword for the book. A mention must also be made of other former National Service men who have prompted memories and given encouragement. They include Alton Douglas (ex 5th Royal Inniskilling Dragoon Guards) and my late cousin Brian Moody (ex-Intelligence Corps).

Of course, fifty years have elapsed since I finished my compulsory two years service and whilst I have done my best to recount the various episodes as I remember them, I hope I may be forgiven for any mistakes which may have crept into the narrative. As William Shakespeare himself once put it, "Old men forget".

FOREWORD

Ever since Alistair Sim and Margaret Rutherford starred in that rumbustious 1950 comedy The Happiest Days Of Your Life many people have accepted the notion, however much they hated school, that it was not so bad in retrospect. The same might be said for those who completed National Service.

After serving their compulsory two years, at the equivalent of 20p a day, most men were more eager to return to civilian life, to carve out a decent career and build up a family, than dwell on their experiences.

Now, in their mature years, they have come to view their time in the Armed Forces objectively. Time has enhanced memories and tended to blunt resentment of an iron discipline to say nothing of boredom and some less pleasant encounters.

Although few might agree that their days in uniform were their 'happiest' days, the period was certainly a highlight in their lives. They also recognise that they were very privileged people. As teenagers they were able to engage in many free adventures and experiences which are denied today's generation.

When manpower was a critical factor in military operations the National Serviceman was there at the sharp end. In an era where garrisons of British Forces were strung out around the globe, youngsters at their most impressionable and formative years were plucked from the comfort of their homes and plunged into an alien world in which they had to mix with people from different backgrounds. It was a profound shock. Almost overnight boys became men who returned home frequently bronzed by the sun of foreign lands.

Therefore it is not surprising that these memories, to say nothing of bonds of friendship and support - as well as their identity number - remained with them for life.

Many will also admit that the discipline they resented so much stood them in good stead for the future. It is natural that they should compare themselves to today's youth.

Some National Servicemen like Alan Brewin made the most of the unique opportunities offered in a strange land amid unusual people and occasionally facing apparently insurmountable challenges. But, as an accomplished linguist, he approached his task with the enthusiasm of Hannibal crossing the Alps, rose in the ranks, and won respect despite inexplicable hostility from some career soldiers.

Thankfully, many former National Servicemen like Alan Brewin have decided to record their experiences and provide an insight into every day life in the Army in the mid-1950's.

This highly entertaining account is a valuable record because, given a smaller and wholly professional volunteer Army equipped with greater firepower and technology, it is unlikely that we will see the 1950's version of National Serviceman again.

Lt. Colonel Aubrey Chalmers,
Warwickshire County President,
The Royal British Legion.

INTRODUCTION

Between 1947 and 1960 some two million young men were conscripted into the Armed Forces to do National Service and of these 1,132,872 served in the Army. They were involved, along with regulars, in campaigns and battles around the World in Aden, Cyprus, Egypt, Korea and Malaya. There were 2,912 servicemen killed in these campaigns, of whom 395 were National Servicemen.

2003 sees the fortieth anniversary of the end of National Service the last man having been discharged in 1963. It is also the fiftieth anniversary of the completion of the author's own full time service in November 1953.

"Enter Drum and Colours", in addition to being a Shakespearian stage direction, describes the author's own military experiences. "The Drum" signifies the JTC band at school and the associated cadet service which helped to prepare the author for his full time service. "The Colours" signifies the two years full time period of National Service which was followed by time with the TA.

The book is very much a personal account of how one young man came to terms with compulsory military service and the experiences endured or enjoyed.

Alan Brewin
Nov 2003

Regimental Depot, The Green Howards, Richmond, North Yorkshire.

CHAPTER 1

RICHMOND, YORKSHIRE

The train rolled slowly into Richmond station finally coming to a halt in a cloud of steam. Voices shouted, doors slammed as I gathered up my belongings and looked apprehensively out on to the platform. It was 1st November, 1951 and this was the first day of my two years National Service. I stepped out and noticed other young men up and down the train were putting in an appearance. There were several uniformed NCO's immaculate in sharply creased battledress and blindingly polished boots strutting up and down the platform shouting incomprehensible commands. A burly sergeant, wearing the red sash worn by senior NCO's and Warrant Officers in infantry regiments of the line, bore down upon me. "Are you for The Green Howards?" "Yes" I managed to reply, "outside and into the truck", he snapped. As I left the station, I noticed other lads were joining NCO's in Royal Signals and Royal Armoured Corps trucks bound for Catterick. Outside stood a camouflaged Bedford 3 tonner. Being interested in transport I knew this was a Bedford QL TCV (Troop Carrying Vehicle), known to the army as "screamers" because of the high pitch whine from their permanently engaged 4-Wheel Drive. I scrambled into the back alongside a lad wearing a University scarf which I recognised as Birmingham University's. "Are you from Brum?" I asked, and he gave me a surprised answer "Yes – are you?" Other young men were climbing into the truck which had a white line painted about two feet inside with the words "Load forward of this line". We all obediently crammed into the front end of the truck onto wooden benches. The sergeant got into the cab with the driver and we were off.

Richmond was, and still is, a sleepy little Yorkshire town with a cobbled square and an obelisk monument in the centre of the square. We climbed steeply up a hill and, turning a corner, passed the War Memorial to 'Green Howards' who lost their lives during the first World War. High up on the outskirts of the town stood the Regimental Depot of the Green Howards. We rumbled past the guardroom and came to a halt. The sergeant appeared again. "Right, everybody out and get fell in". We shambled into some sort of line, clutching small bags and personal possessions. Some wore old clothes, some sports coats and flannels, most wore a tie and one brave soul sported his best navy blue three-piece suit with waistcoat. Our sergeant, who wore the shoulder flashes of The Green Howards, turned away as another even more imposing figure approached. He was a sergeant in The Scots Guards, with black and gold peaked cap, a bristling moustache and a drill stick in his hand. Every button, badge and collardog gleamed in the autumn light, and the creases in his trousers were sharp enough to shave with. (I was to learn that all drill sergeants of The Green Howards were in fact seconded from the Brigade of Guards ensuring The Green Howards were extremely smart on parade.)

"You are the latest intake and I am Sergeant Kerridge, your platoon drill sergeant". He was joined by a corporal and a lance corporal wearing 'Green Howards' flashes. The sergeant continued. "You should know I am the f….. Fuhrer here" and he continued, nodding at the corporal, "this is Corporal Allis who is the Little Fuhrer", the Lance Corporal apparently did not warrant a mention. We later found out his name was Benton and he was a National Service man like ourselves who had been promoted to Lance Corporal. Being responsible for our training, he kept his distance but we gradually got to know him and it was of course the regular corporal (Little Fuhrer) who gave us the hardest time. We all stood dumbstruck at this friendly greeting, the sergeant continued "We have a lot to get through in basic training and, having me as your sergeant, we shall of course be the best platoon. Any questions so far?" "No sergeant" we replied, except for one poor chap who answered "No Sir". "DON'T CALL ME SIR CALL ME SERGEANT", was the immediate thunderous reply. "You play ball with me and I'll play ball with you", he went on "you can either do things the easy way or the hard way. The easy way ain't easy and the hard way's f….. hard. Do I make myself clear". "Yes sergeant", this time we all chorused. "Right, Corporal, take this horrible shower of civvies away I don't want to see them again until they look like soldiers". After that, it was off to the barrack room, which was to be our home till Christmas. We had been told not to bring possessions so there was little to put away, soon our clothes would be parcelled and sent home. We each grabbed a bed all of which were covered by green covers, which we were to learn, had to be taut enough to bounce a coin on. Alongside each bed stood a tall steel cupboard. We then shambled off with our two corporals to draw uniforms and bedding from the stores and equally important, mugs, utensil sets and mess tins. At long last we were dressed in some sort of uniform and marched for the first time to the canteen where we were given a hot meal on large white plates, the mess tins not being needed. During the meal another Green Howards sergeant (we later learned was the Orderly Sergeant) together with the Orderly Officer visited each table and asked "Any Complaints?" We were all far too subdued to do anything but mutter "No sergeant". After the meal we went outside where cookhouse orderlies from the Army Catering Corps had placed two enormous tubs of very hot water. The idea was apparently to use the first tub, which was practically boiling, to wash plates, knives, forks and spoons, and the second cooler tub to rinse them. Heaven help you if you dropped anything in the first tub, it was so deep you stood a good chance of scalding your arm if you tried to fish anything out and you would have had to pay for any replacements out of your National Service pay. The pay in 1951 stood at 4 shillings (20 pence) per day, for which princely sum we were expected to put our lives on the line for our country although most of us were still not old enough to be allowed the vote. We were to discover that we would be marched as a platoon everywhere we went in the depot, including to and from the cookhouse for every meal. The intention was to instil discipline and an *esprit de corps* (it worked).

During the following days we had to pack up personal clothing and possessions in parcels, which were to be sent to our homes. Now we only had army clothing and kit and we seemed to lose our individuality. But on that first night we gradually got to know each other's name and background. Most came from North Yorkshire or County Durham and one or two came from Scotland. I discovered that the chap with the Birmingham University scarf was from Acocks Green and had been deferred to do his National Service because of his University Course. Like me, Johnny Smaller had nominated the RAEC as his preferred unit and because the RAEC did not carry out basic training, we had been sent to Yorkshire to an infantry regiment. Of course the army could have sent us to the Royal Warwickshire Regiment just up the road from Birmingham at Budbrooke Barracks, Warwick but whoever arranged the posting for us was obviously not too strong in the geography department. There was one other new recruit in the platoon who had specified the RAEC as his preferred choice. This was Geoff Barrett, a Chartered Librarian from Skipton who had also been deferred so that he could complete his studies. There was a rich mixture of Northern accents ranging from broad Scots and Geordie to the slightly more intelligible Yorkshire dialect. When bedtime arrived we were very subdued, some almost in tears, missing home comforts and loved ones and trying to come to terms with this new ultra-organised way of life which had been forced upon us for two years. Richmond Barracks stood on a cold and windy high point in North Yorkshire but the old barrack rooms were sturdy brick built edifices surmounted by a clock facing the barrack square and we were reasonably warm with all doors and windows shut, provided we used all our blankets and supplemented them when necessary with greatcoats on our beds.

Over the next day or two we were constantly moved about, drawing further kit, swapping ludicrously over or undersize uniform bits in the stores finally winding up with two complete battledress uniforms, two berets and cap badges, two pairs of heavy matt black ammunition boots and a plethora of webbing belts, straps, ammunition pouches, gaiters and large and small packs. Our uniforms were taken in or altered as necessary by the camp tailor, badges were issued and sewn on and we all had a visit to the camp barber who had obviously been a Yorkshire sheep shearer in an earlier life. Suddenly we began at least to look like soldiers and then began the interminable evenings polishing brasses, blancoing equipment and converting the matt black boots to highly polished items with toecaps like mirrors by means of lashings of black polish "small circles" and spit and polish. There was of course no television and not even a radio was allowed. We were also issued with ID dogtags to wear round our necks day and night and kitbags, which we had to stencil with name, rank and number. The number was to be impressed upon us for life. Every morning beds would be made up and kit laid out in a particular way on beds for inspection by the corporals after the shout "Stand By Your Beds". This invariably resulted in some poor soldier's kit being declared 'mancky' and thrown on the floor or occasionally through a window by the Corporals.

Soon the day arrived when we were paraded before our very own drill sergeant or fuhrer, as he preferred to call himself. Eagle-eyed inspections were followed by hours of marching, practising foot drills, parade orders and salutes. As infantrymen we were now issued by the armoury with Mark IV Lee Enfield rifles, plus bayonets and steel helmets (I couldn't imagine ever actually using the bayonet). The Mark IV Lee Enfield rifles (originally introduced in 1941) were almost identical to those used by the school JTC and I was already well used to handling them, drilling with them and cleaning them. At school we had each been allocated a rifle, all of which were kept chained up in a locked armoury which was opened on Thursdays ("Corps day") for us to use and on Saturday mornings for us to clean and oil our rifles for inspection. Being in the Corps Band, it was also necessary for me to white blanco all sorts of equipment including ceremonial belt, gaiters, drum cords and gauntlets. All this had to be fitted in on Saturdays in addition to periods of sixth form education.

Arms drill in the Green Howards became our way of life till we collapsed exhausted after a day of square-bashing. After tea we would spend the evening 'bulling' boots, and trying to fit in baths or washes (there were no showers).

The pressure on recruits never slackened from the time our feet hit the floor at Reveille to the time we crawled into bed at "Lights out".

Arranging a routine for personal hygiene proved a most difficult task. There were not enough washbasins, loos or baths for all the members of the barrack room to use simultaneously and time was precious in the morning between Reveille and breakfast. Some overcame the problem by getting up earlier and earlier and trying to shave before Reveille in the dark. Others would try to squeeze in a much needed bath before being paraded for an evening meal. I found myself in serious trouble for sneaking into the "ablutions" one morning after the corporal had declared them polished and clean awaiting the daily inspection by the sergeant. On another occasion, having just managed to fit in a five minute bath, I had insufficient time to make an entry in the bath book recording the bath before being marched off to tea. The Little Fuhrer, having seen me coming out of the bathroom, inevitably reported me to the Sergeant Fuhrer for not signing the bath book.

In due course I was put on a charge and marched in before my Company Commander for the serious offence of "failing to record a bath in the bath book".

When eventually I stood before him he studied the charge sheet (commonly known as a "fizzer" or a "252") with some surprise. He was a 2nd Lieutenant in the Green Howards, not much older than me, and either National Service or on a Short Service Commission. His sympathies were very obviously with me and I was let off with a warning to comply with such paperwork in the future without any form of punishment. This, of course, left the Little Fuhrer looking rather silly for putting me on a charge and I was somewhat apprehensive about my future dealings with him. I have to say in all fairness I was not victimised in any way.

Parades were enlivened by all the usual jokey comments from our two corporals who slept each night in a partitioned-off area in our barrack room. Our sergeant continued to drill us and on about day five he asked me "Have you shaved this morning Brewin?" "No sergeant", I replied, "Why not?" he bellowed "Because my beard grows very slowly and I've only just started shaving", I said very bravely. "In future you will shave every morning and if you have no beard, you will go through the motions", came his reply. This "go through the motions" was a favourite line whether we were on the parade ground, in our barracks or engaged on weapons training. Other favourite comments included "I shall move you and your feet won't touch", "Get a grip lad", said quietly and menacingly to some unfortunate recruit and "You are all marching like pregnant f..... camels". An unforgivable crime was to try to shuffle into a correct position after being given the command "HALT". Such movement was invariably noticed and would give rise to an almost hysterical shriek from the drill sergeant "RIGHT OR WRONG STAND STILL".

At the end of the second week, an Armistice Day Parade had been arranged, including a march to the War Memorial. A few days before, the Depot RSM, a figure slightly akin to God and far more fearsome than the officers, addressed us on parade. He explained we would march downhill to the War Memorial after a CO's inspection to check our turn out, we would not slip going downhill, we would not lose step, it was a solemn occasion, and we would be remembering all the men of the Regiment who had gone before, including those who had fallen in two World Wars. We would, of course, be upholding the honour of the Regiment by being immaculate. After this pep talk everyone frantically polished, bulled and ironed everything in sight, especially our best battledress uniforms. The day dawned, the parade was held, a Regimental bugler played The Last Post and Reveille and we were marched back to barracks. We were then called for a parade before the RSM. There were several platoons each having thirty young soldiers and we waited apprehensively for the dressing down and inevitable catalogue of mistakes. There was a long silence, the RSM stood stock still, his World War II medals gleaming on his chest whilst he looked at our young faces. "Well done" he said at last, "Bloody good show. Parade dismiss". These were the first words of praise we had heard since entering the barrack gates and were even more appreciated coming from the Great Man himself.

He was not always so patient with young officers. One day we were drilling on the vast parade ground when a young subaltern appeared from the Officers' Mess. The RSM, who was on the other side of the parade ground, saluted but the young, recently-commissioned, lad did not notice. "I'm saluting you Sir", bellowed the RSM from what appeared to be about 100 yards away. The young officer paused, his face went pale and he eventually saluted, somewhat shakily, "Carry on Sarnt Major" he managed to croak whilst about two hundred young soldiers watched and smirked at his discomfort. Major parades were taken by the CO who appeared occasionally from the Officers' Mess at the top of the steps to the Parade Ground before descending followed by his Labrador dog. Having been minutely inspected by Corporals, Sergeants and Sergeant Majors before he put in his appearance we knew our kit and turn out was A1, but we were always nervous if the CO and the dog paused before us in case the dog mistook the rigidly stationary brown clad legs for trees. Fortunately, he never did.

The day dawned when we were required to attend the MO's sanctuary for injections and immunisations against all manner of illnesses including Typhoid, Paratyphoid, Yellow Fever, TB and Tetanus all of which were done on the same morning. Army Books AB64, which we always carried, served as ID documents, paybooks and proof of our injections and medical assessments, known to soldiers as PULHEEMS (Part I served as an identity document whilst Part II served as a paybook). I understood from a friend in the RAF that they were given half a day to recover from all their injections, our Drill Sergeant had other ideas and we were given half-an-hour rifle drill "to get the blood moving" to quote the Fuhrer's words. Amazingly, no-one actually fell over although some were very close to it.

We also managed to cross the RSM as a platoon. Apparently some imbecile went into the indoor rifle range in the evening laid out all his kit on the floor and heavily blancoed both the kit and the surrounding floor area. The RSM, having looked in last thing at night, had the two corporals, who slept in a partitioned off area at the end of the barrack room, out of bed to show them the state of the floor. They in turn reported to the Fuhrer who was in the sergeants' Mess. He arrived when we lay in bed exhausted after a long day's square bashing, had us all up and dressed in denim overalls and we then had to clean the entire length of the indoor range. We eventually got to bed well after midnight. No-one ever claimed responsibility for messing up the range but certainly everyone was very careful about cleaning up after blancoing, wherever they were after that.

After some weeks of square bashing and training in the gym we moved on to weapon training. Reveille was normally 06.00 hours, but we were told by the Little Fuhrer that the following day it would be 05.00 hours. We struggled sleepily into uniform, had breakfast and were paraded outside to go to the outdoor range. As we stood awaiting transport, a small convoy of trucks appeared with RASC drivers. We stood, already cold in the pitch dark of a Yorkshire early morning when it suddenly dawned on us that instead of our familiar Green Howards' Bedford QL's with canopies and benches, we were going to be taken in Austin Loadstar open 3 tonners with no shelter and virtually nowhere to sit. We all scrambled on to the trucks and set off to the range, which turned out to be at Catterick. It was a cold, dark and extremely uncomfortable journey across the moors but eventually we arrived and were left hanging about till about 09.00 hours when it was actually light enough to see the targets. I did not have much difficulty on the range. During my four years cadet experience I had qualified as a first class shot at the Kingsbury army range on .303 rifles and, in fact, I had already shot on the Yorkshire range in 1948 when I was camping with the school JTC at Catterick. I had also trained in the Cadets with the ever reliable Bren LMG (Light Machine Gun) and the 9mm Sten Gun, (a light automatic gun designed at short notice in World War II to utilise captured German ammunition and a not very accurate weapon). Those who had never held a rifle before, however, suffered severe bruising from the kickback to the shoulder through not holding the rifle tightly enough. At long last we headed back to our barracks on our draughty trucks. Before our well earned hot meal we had to clean and oil the rifles we had used to the Corporal's satisfaction. This was followed after tea by more hours of cleaning equipment, pressing clothes and bulling boots. One day, word spread, a mobile canteen would be on hand after weapon training. There was much speculation and imaginative young men had visions of attractive girls serving exotic food and drink. Sadly the reality turned out to be a small Church Army mobile canteen, manned by a kindly lady of advanced years, serving tea (much appreciated) in thick white mugs.

At long last after weeks in barracks we were told we could attend a Saturday dance over the County boundary in Darlington, County Durham. Transport (covered QL's) would be provided but heaven help anyone who missed the trucks back to barracks. Arriving outside the dance hall, I was approached by a very pretty girl who asked whether I would like to take her to the dance for the evening. I could not believe my good fortune and fumbled in my battledress pockets to find enough cash to get us both through the door. Sadly, once inside, my escort vanished never to be seen again. Bewildered, I stood there whilst a more worldly NCO explained that all girls had to be escorted to be allowed in to avoid the possibility of local tarts and trollops picking up young soldiers. I had probably had a lucky escape, as the girl who had come in with me was apparently well known to the Military Police. She would be looking for someone of more senior rank with money to burn. Eventually, after an enjoyable evening with pals from the barracks and other more respectable girls, from nearby hospitals, we made our way back to barracks and military routine once more took over.

Each night as we cleaned our kit, we found out a little more about each other. Mac, the burly Scot, was a fanatical Rangers supporter. As he polished his brasses, he would sing in a strong Scottish accent to the tune of "The Red Flag" – "Oh Charlie Shaw, he never saw where Alan Moreton puit the barl. He puit the barl into the net and Charlie Shaw lee down an gret. Oh Charlie Shaw, he never saw where Alan Morton puit the barl." This would be followed by more Rangers songs and jokes, each one becoming more anti-Celtic. A typical joke was "Why do Rangers have the best chant?" Answer: "Because it is easier to keep shouting F..... the Pope than F..... the Moderator of the Assembly of the Free Church of Scotland". The Protestant/Catholic antipathy in Glasgow revealed was an eye opener to me. This football generated religious division caused some of us to worry we might have Catholic recruits in our intake who would be upset. A quiet word to Mac, who was not in reality at all anti-Catholic, ensured future singing and jokes would not give offence. This was a good example of the platoon pulling together. (An interesting sidelight on National Service was the fact that most young men who registered in Northern Ireland were never called up for National Service, the government of the day believing that such a move would be seen as provocative by the Irish Nationalist section of the community. Nor did the government as a general rule call up members of the ethnic minority communities, which were much smaller in the 1950's, so the vast majority of recruits were white English, Scots and Welsh young men).

Other recruits spoke of their families, friends and interests. None were married but many were missing girl friends and fiancées. The evenings were enlivened by visits from the corporals who would pour contempt on our pathetic attempts to bring our uniforms and kit up to the same standard as theirs. The corporals were members of that mysterious body, The Depot's Permanent Staff. The Permanent Staff included the cooks who prepared our food daily and served it with big spoons and ladles as we queued hungrily in line. The food often seemed to bear little, if any, resemblance to the ambitious menu set up daily on a blackboard by the Cook Sergeant, but in army terms it was pretty good if not exactly home cooking. The Permanent Staff also included the Regimental Police who made up a private mafia force for the RSM. Unlike the Military Police Redcaps, they were members of the Green Howards Regiment who wore RP armbands and zealously manned the guardroom and entrance to the barracks. When we were eventually allowed out of the barracks it was necessary to pass the guardroom which had a verandah outside constantly patrolled by an RP. There was also a full length mirror at the guardroom surmounted by the legend "Are you properly dressed". Heaven help you if you passed this mirror with a button undone, or without a webbing belt suitably blancoed and brassoed, you would be insulted and probably put on a charge.

I soon fell in with Johnny Smaller and Geoff Barrett, and in fact we were to stay together for the next two years. Johnny Smaller unfortunately had the Christian names John Thomas, one of the many terms, I was to learn, used in the army for the male organ. Of course the corporals took great pleasure on parade in addressing Johnny "One pace forward Smaller John Thomas" and Johnny would have to obey stoney faced whilst the corporals sniggered at their scintillating wit. Whilst Geoff was a studious young man, with glasses, the very epitome of a librarian. Johnny was a gregarious confident young student, a trumpet player and jazz fanatic whose heroine was Ella Fitzgerald. Both of them were about three years older than me having been deferred to complete their studies.

Eventually Christmas approached and we looked forward to the completion of our basic training and Christmas leave. One day our Sergeant Fuhrer came into our barrack room. Geoff, Johnny and I were hard at work cleaning equipment but no-one else happened to be there. Our Sergeant quietly spoke to us "You three lads are all moving on to the RAEC Depot. If you play your cards right you'll all wind up sergeant-instructors and you are still only youngsters. Think about signing on because you've got a flying start". We were amazed. Not only had he spoken to us like equals, but he thought we had the making of professional soldiers. In fact, despite his fearsome greeting when we arrived, he had proved to be a very fair but firm NCO and we were not subject to the ludicrous bullying or "beasting" suffered by some of my contemporaries who trained with other regiments. The constant fear whilst doing basic training was that we would fail to meet standards and be put back for another spell of training. Fortunately all our platoon passed out satisfactorily first time without the need for what was called "backsquadding".

Towards the end of our basic training we were each seen by the PSO (Personnel Selection Officer) at an office adjoining the Orderly Room. This was considered to be a good "skive" as it meant our endless square bashing was stopped for an hour or two for individual members of the platoon to be interviewed. The majority of local recruits were destined to remain with the Regiment for the rest of their National Service but quite a few were being assessed for other units or regiments in which they had shown an interest. When my turn came, the officer carrying out the interview made particular reference to my education, my languages and my cadet experience. "Why opt for the Educational Corps?", I was asked. The officer went on to say the army was seeking recruits with a knowledge of foreign languages for further training in the Russian language. There was a possibility of a twelve month Cambridge course and the option to proceed to a WOSB or War Office Selection Board for Officers. With my cadet experience I would almost certainly be commissioned into the Intelligence Corps especially if I was prepared to sign on for a three year short service commission after which I would be free to return to civilian life. This was a most unexpected and flattering offer and was one of those crossroads which sometimes suddenly appear in life. Perhaps, foolishly, I opted to retain the RAEC as my first choice which would mean promotion to Sergeant rather than Officer status but I would only have to do two years full-time service, not three. After school years at KES where my whole life had revolved around English, French, German and Spanish studies I was not ready to take on yet more years of studying a totally new language. "It's your decision", said the PSO, "The RAEC it shall be." I later found out that both Geoff's and Johnny's applications to transfer to the RAEC had been confirmed. The three of us would be going to Beaconsfield.

At long last having virtually completed our basic training we were sent off with railway warrants on Christmas leave. My father, mother and sister were so glad to see me and my friends wanted to know all about army life. Why, I thought, did they always first ask "When are you going back?" when I had only just come home. All went well till Christmas Eve when I was horrified to receive a telegram "Report back to Richmond Barracks". What on earth was going on? There were very few trains on Christmas Day and in any case my family was expecting me to share Christmas with them after all my hard training. I agonised. Should I try to get back Christmas Day or leave it to Boxing Day, or even the day after? What if the Military Police came round to arrest me as AWOL or worse, as a deserter? After a family conference a course of action was agreed. I would use my warrant to travel back on Boxing Day from Birmingham New Street after spending Christmas Day with the family. And so I finally arrived at the Regimental Depot late on Boxing Day. The barracks were deserted but there were two Regimental Police on duty who sent me to the Orderly Office. There the duty corporal was surprised to see me. The telegram had been intended to arrive the day after Boxing Day but the corporal going off duty on Christmas Eve had sent it off in an unusual display of efficiency. They had sent me the telegram to remind me I was still in The Green Howards and not yet transferred to the RAEC At this point, the orderly officer came in and overheard the end of our conversation. As the barracks were empty, he offered to show me the Regimental Museum and give me an overview of the Regiment's history. This seemed a much more interesting way of passing the time than sitting in an empty barrack room. I did explain I was shortly to leave the Regiment but he replied "No matter, you should find out more about us before you go". And so it was I discovered what a splendid Regiment I had trained with. Many of my intake were destined to fight communists in the jungles of what was then Malaya, sadly, not all Green Howards would come back. More poppies for the Green Howards' memorial which still stands in Richmond, though the Depot is now a housing estate.

CHAPTER 2

WILTON PARK, BEACONSFIELD

It was January 1952 and, my basic training completed I received my posting instructions from the Orderly Office at Richmond Barracks, together with the usual railway warrant. I was to report to the Army School of Education and RAEC Depot at Wilton Park, Beaconsfield. I packed all my kit and said goodbye to the rest of the platoon. It seemed a long time since the beginning of November when we had all arrived with such apprehension as civilians and now I was leaving the barracks as a soldier. Johnny and Geoff were also to be posted to Beaconsfield but my orders had already arrived so I made my way alone to the station. It was necessary to travel first of all to London and it was late in the evening when I eventually arrived at Marylebone. I managed to get something to eat at the station buffet. In the 1950's, all main line stations had an office for servicemen known as the RTO and I reported only to be told there was no train to Beaconsfield until the milk train very early next morning. I went to the waiting room which was still warm and settled down as best I could to get a few hours sleep on a padded bench. It seemed that no sooner had I dozed off than my shoulder was being shaken. I woke to find a railway porter standing over me. "Sorry to wake you, lad" he said "but we have to empty the waiting room at night and lock it up till 6 a.m." "Can't I stay?", I said "No" he replied "It's to stop the tramps and down and outs using us every night as a doss house". Sleepily, I gathered up my kit and moved on to the platform. It was very cold and a few snowflakes were drifting under the big glass canopy. I found a hard bench, settled down again and turned up the collar of my greatcoat to keep out the cold, whilst I waited for the milk train. Suddenly there was a shout and I turned to find two Military Police striding towards me, immaculate with red caps and white blancoed belts and gaiters. "Stand to attention" said the older corporal, whilst the younger stolid lance corporal stood behind him. "What are you on?" he enquired. This was a common question in the army meaning "What are you doing?" I resisted the temptation to say "on a bench" and explained I was in transit to Beaconsfield waiting for a train. He looked at my Green Howards cap badge. "What are you doing there". I explained I was going for an instructor course. "You realise you are improperly dressed. You should not have your greatcoat collar turned up." "I thought it was allowed in inclement weather,

Corporal" I said. He looked at me and said "You could wind up as a sergeant couldn't you?". "Yes Corporal". "Right turn your collar down and carry on" he said, marching off. As they moved away I heard the Neanderthal lance corporal say "What's in-f.....-clement Corporal?". I guessed the corporal felt our paths might cross after I had become a sergeant and decided to leave me in peace.

When I arrived at Wilton Park (the RAEC Depot) there was a very long drive to walk up with all my kit till eventually I reached the barrier and guardroom. I produced my movement order and was sent to the Orderly Office who sent me on to my new billet. This turned out to be in the stables and out-buildings of the stately home which now served as the Officers' Mess. Soon Geoff, Johnny and I were reunited and joined other members of our new platoon. Most were older than me having been deferred until they had completed first or sometimes even second Degrees at University. The atmosphere was different however. In the Green Howards there had been a general acceptance of National Service as a necessary evil and there was a bonding often found in the infantry. Any recruit struggling with kit or ironing or boots would be helped by other members of the platoon so that we all passed basic training and nobody was backsquadded. There were several new entrants from other infantry regiments with this same outlook but there were also older more frustrated men from other units who constantly carped about what a waste of time the whole army business was. They intended to do the minimum possible, try to obtain home postings, and go home every weekend. I could imagine them in the future in civilian life bickering in some common room about the Headmaster and I tended to pal up with the 18 and 19 year old soldiers in the platoon together with my friends from The Green Howards. The next day we met our new boss. Instead of a sergeant in the Scots Guards, we now had a company sergeant major in the Welsh Guards. CSM Taffy Morgan was a fiery warrant officer who also sported a fine moustache. In fact we found him a very decent CSM who tolerated these strange, National Service would-be instructors whilst we gradually fitted into a new regime and learned something of man management.

We were faced with a two months training programme designed to make us capable of instructing soldiers and getting them through Army Certificates of Education, Grade I, II and III. These Certificates were needed by humble privates and NCO's to enable them to qualify for promotion at various levels. The RAEC also dealt with other educational services, including the operation of Command Libraries, the supplying of Unit Libraries for recreational purposes and the provision to commissioned officers of the courses and books they needed to pass Staff College examinations for senior staff appointments. RAEC sergeants would also be required to carry out the usual military duties of a senior NCO wherever they were posted.

CSM Morgan was responsible for our military training and parades were still held every morning. After a few days we were moved to a World War II Nissen Hut which was to be our barrack room and home for the next two months. It was fairly cold and cheerless but there was a large woodburning stove in the centre we soon activated which tended to be the focal point round which we would gather. There was also a floor which needed polishing with a "bumper" and we would skate around the floor with dusters round our boots before room inspection. Whilst kit inspections and parades still occurred regularly, the atmosphere was much more relaxed, more like a college gathering than an infantry platoon barrack room. We were actually allowed evenings in the NAAFI where Bill, a six foot former student, would entertain us with jazz and pop music on an old piano in the corner whilst we were served by good-natured NAAFI girls who put up with a lot of jokes and comments. High above the serving hatch was a large wall mounted radio loudspeaker and it was through this speaker one night in February 1952 we heard King George VI had died and young Princess Elizabeth was now our Queen. Suddenly we had become Her Majesty's Forces and King's Regulations had become Queen's Regulations.

A story circulated in the camp that one evening, CSM Morgan had looked into the NAAFI whilst Bill Doherty was playing the piano as usual. "We need you tomorrow to play for a Sergeants' Mess function Doherty", he announced. "Yes Sir", said Doherty. The Sergeant Major went on "I also need two others with an interest in music for the same function." Several would-be instructors and graduates struggled for the honour. "I was in the School Orchestra", said one, whilst another, even more superior, said "Actually, I have a degree in Music." "Splendid", said the CSM "You two can push the piano up to the Sergeants' Mess when the NAAFI closes and push it back again tomorrow when it re-opens". This was a classic example of the old army adage, "Never volunteer".

Although there were benefits at Beaconsfield there were also disadvantages. There was a tight roster for regimental duties, including Fire Picket Duty and Guardroom Duty, which seemed to come round all too frequently. These duties in the Green Howards had been carried out by the Regimental Police and other Permanent Staff. Now we were expected to fit in such duties alongside our training courses. Both Fire Picket and Guard Duty involved long hours night and day at the gate, patrolling the perimeter and checking all the buildings spread throughout the camp. We worked two hours on and two hours off and were then expected bright and early on parade the following morning for a full day's work. On those cold January nights we would parade for CSM Morgan to inspect us in our best battledress, greatcoats fully buttoned up with webbing belts outside, before being launched into the dark and cold on our nightly checks. We worked in pairs and usually managed to spend at least twenty minutes opening and checking the camp chapel which was warm, inviting and quiet at night.

One day I recognised an old friend based in an adjoining Nissen Hut. It was Don Yetman who had studied modern languages with me in the Sixth Form at King Edward's Birmingham. Don was an excellent musician and had served with me in the school JTC Corps of Drums. Don had been a solo bugler whilst I had been one of two tenor drummers. When CSM Morgan discovered Don's musical talent, Don was given the job of duty bugler which meant he had to get up even earlier than the rest of us although at least he did not have to do the dreaded guard duties and fire picket duties. Soon another well known face appeared. This was another Old Edwardian and former JTC Member whom I shall call "X". Even at school and despite four years service in the Corps, "X" could never keep step when marching and persisted in swinging his left arm forward instead of his right when stepping off with his left foot on the parade ground, much to the annoyance of the NCO in charge. This habit spread chaos in the ranks as other people thought they were out of step and tried to follow him. Eventually "X", who had an excellent academic brain at KES was taken off such parades and given other necessary but menial fatigues to carry out. In addition to spud bashing these included cleaning the various toilets and removing such unofficial notices as "Stand Closer, it's shorter than you think". Other notices officially posted included "Do not throw cigarette butts into the urinals" to which someone had helpfully added "They are so difficult to smoke when soggy". On another occasion I glimpsed "X" single-handedly and black as the ace of spades, unloading a ten ton truck load of coal with a spade.

Johnny Smaller also now revealed his musical capabilities. From somewhere he had borrowed a trumpet to entertain us. Unfortunately he could only play one tune – "I'll be Around", and every time in the last forty years I have heard this jazz standard, my mind goes back to evenings in the NAAFI at Beaconsfield.

Our courses included Educational Psychology, Adult Education and Teaching Practices, which we fitted in with parades and instruction in regimental duties. We knew we were being constantly assessed by officers and warrant officers. We knew that if we failed we would be RTU or Returned To Unit, which in my case would have involved a trip back to

Richmond and the Green Howards. We were now all privates in the RAEC with new cap badges, shoulder flashes and district flashes on our arms.

One day our officer instructor threw a problem at us. We were required to stand before about thirty other aspiring instructors and address them on any subject for five minutes without preparation but using blackboard or any visual aids to hand. The first private to be selected was a Maths graduate and he spent his five minutes proving Pythagoras' theorem on the blackboard. The second was an English graduate who spoke of the importance of Shakespeare in English Literature. It was then my turn. I had been impressed (but slightly bored) with my predecessors. I decided to speak on the design and development of post war public service vehicles. I illustrated the talk with chalk drawings of half cab, full fronted and underfloor-engined vehicles and a list of chassis makers and body builders. Most of those assembled did at least sit up to see what on earth I was doing but I was aware it had not been very academic. I was surprised to find later my score had in fact been pretty high.

After a couple of weeks we were told we could have a 48 hour pass at the weekend. This was the first such pass ever offered to me since joining the army the previous year. There was a problem however. With pay at only 4/- per day I could not afford the train fare home. I resolved to hitchhike and set off in uniform with a few things in my small pack. Although it was very common for motorists to pick up servicemen in the 1950's, it took me almost half-an-hour to obtain my first lift, which turned out to be an eightwheeler BRS lorry. I climbed into the cab but the roar of the engine, which lay between me and the driver, made conversation difficult. The lorry trundled along slowly and eventually I was dropped off in Oxford, still miles from my destination in Birmingham. I suddenly realised I was quite likely to spend the whole of my leave travelling up and down the roads. Then my luck changed! A Jaguar Mk V Saloon speeding towards me pulled up about 50 yards past and I ran down the road. The passenger window was wound down and the passenger, a very attractive girl, asked me where I was heading. "Birmingham", I replied. "You're in luck, so are we, hop in" she said, and I opened the back door of the car. The driver, a middle-aged man, grunted "Mind those boots on the seats" and I was in and we were off. As the speedometer went ever higher, I sat in the middle of the back seat amongst opulent leather and walnut, counting my blessings, watching the world hurtle past and the speedo heading towards the magic 100mph. The girl in the front turned and chatted to me and gradually I realised she was a stewardess with British European Airways and the driver was a BEA Captain. We sped towards Elmdon Airport, Birmingham and eventually I was dropped on the Outer Circle Route to finish my journey by bus. I watched the Jaguar drive off, envying the driver his car, his job and his companion. My family were so pleased to see me but of course I was soon due back. Fortunately Dad paid my rail fare back to Beaconsfield but I mentally resolved it was just too far and too stressful to spend any future weekend passes hitchhiking home.

As we worked further through our training programmes I realised I would probably not want to make my future civilian career as a teacher or lecturer, but I was willing to finish the course and complete my National Service as an Instructor if only I could pass out at the end of the course.

One weekend, I went into High Wycombe on a Saturday and found there was a dance on that night at the Town Hall. I turned up in the evening and found there was also a large contingent of young men from the Royal Armoured Corps stationed nearby together with some RAF types. I had a few dances with a very pretty girl called Penny who had a cutglass accent, and I noticed a tough looking soldier from the Armoured Corps also danced with her. About half-way through the evening she asked me what I was doing the following day (which was a Sunday). Apparently there was going to be a little party at her home. I was surprised but said I could come over during the day. She then invited me to her house which had an extremely expensive sounding address in Chalfont St Giles. "Will this be OK with your parents?" I asked apprehensively. She smiled, "Absolutely no problem". The next day I spent the early morning trying to look my best then set off in uniform on a tortuous journey, eventually arriving at lunch time. It was indeed an imposing house with beautiful gardens and, as I approached the door, Penny came out to meet me looking very glamorous. This all seemed like a dream. What was I doing at a family party in this super house with a girl who did not even know me?

We went into the house and all gradually became clear. After introducing me to her kindly parents, I looked to see who the other friends were she had mentioned. The first person I saw was the tough looking Royal Armoured Corps trooper and there were two other servicemen from the army and the RAF both of whom had been at the dance at High Wycombe. Fortunately Penny had two sisters and we were all served wonderful food from the kitchen of this magnificent house. The RAC trooper, who had been glowering at me all night at High Wycombe, turned out to be a very decent lad. He came over to me. "This is a rum do and no mistake. I thought Penny wanted me to take her out and it's more like a vicar's teaparty" he said. I explained that I too had thought I was going to be the only serviceman there, but we all enjoyed ourselves and thanked

Penny and her family, especially her Mum who had had the idea of a lunch party for young National Servicemen far from home. I managed to get a lift most of the way back to Beaconsfield and walked up that long drive at Wilton Park in time to go back on duty. Sadly I never saw Penny again.

As I had not been home since the first 48 hour pass, I would occasionally phone home from a red telephone box in Beaconsfield. Telephones had been few and far between in the years immediately after the War, but after being on a lengthy waiting list, we had been granted a shared line at home. Now Mum and Dad actually had a private telephone of their own which made it easier to keep in touch.

Some time later I saw an advertisement for another dance to be held at the Town Hall in High Wycombe. Remembering the great time I had had after meeting Penny I felt I must go again. Although Penny was not to be seen I immediately noticed a striking looking girl with high cheek bones, blonde hair, blue eyes and, as I soon found out, an intriguing Scandinavian accent. We spent most of the evening together and I discovered Anja, for that was her name, was a Finnish au pair who was living with a family in Gerrards Cross. Her family back home ran a hotel in Punkaharju and she was working in England to improve her English after a spell in Paris to improve her French before joining the family business back in Finland. For the rest of my time at the RAEC depot we met each weekend, once at her Gerrards Cross home, once in Uxbridge and other times in Beaconsfield. I bought myself a copy of Marlborough's "Finnish Self Taught" from a bookshop in High Wycombe but found it a most difficult language to learn. Anja laughed when she saw me studying "Marlborough." "I will teach you all the Finnish you need," she said "your first lesson is the Finnish word for 'darling' which is 'rakas' and you can start all your letters to me with this word." Back at Wilton Park, I was approaching the end of the course and Geoff, Johnny and I were relieved and gratified to find we had all qualified as instructors, leading to automatic immediate promotion to sergeant.

Promotion gave us the necessary authority to use the Sergeants' Mess. We could not believe we could now use the same bar as the sergeants and sergeant majors who had drilled and pressured us through two months of training. We still however lived and slept in our World War II Nissen Huts. One substantial benefit was that we now ceased to be rostered for guard duty, fire pickets and other regimental chores. These were now the responsibility of the new intake starting a new course as privates. We were shortly due for a week's leave before we were sent "into the field" to quote our instructing officer. First, however, our future destinations had to be decided. In the 1950's the British Army spanned the globe. There was a massive presence in Germany with BAOR and many available postings in colonies and other territories world wide, including Aden, Cyprus, Hong Kong, Malta, Malaya etc. We did, however, discover there were three vacancies in Tripoli, Libya and Geoff, Johnny and I decided to put in for them. We were pleased to hear in due course that our postings were indeed to Tripoli. Before we left Beaconsfield, there were more goodbyes to new and old colleagues. Most had passed the course but a few were being 'Returned to Unit' as unsuitable instructor material. Don Yetman, the bugler turned instructor had passed and was off to Gibraltar as a sergeant. On our last night in the Sergeants' Mess, we met for a farewell drink. There was a knock at the door and the Guard Commander in best battledress appeared asking for me. "There's a young lady at the gate without a pass asking for you" he said. As I followed him to the barrier I knew who would be there. It was a tearful Anja who had walked up the long dark drive to see me on my last evening. We were all confined to camp until we had been cleared and kitted out for overseas but the Guard Commander turned a blind eye as I walked Anja down that long drive back to safety and a bus ride back to Gerrards Cross. We talked over our happy times and agreed to keep in touch whilst I

was overseas in Libya. Anja was shortly to return to Scandinavia and somehow it seemed it might be difficult to meet again. I returned to the Mess very subdued despite all the jokes I had to take. The next day we drew all our tropical kit, including three sets of KD shirts, shorts and long trousers, new badges, hose tops, wrap round ankle puttees, and other miscellaneous bits and pieces. Then it was off for a week's embarkation leave with the usual travel warrants thus avoiding the need for hitchhiking.

Leave gave me the chance to visit friends and relatives, but when I dropped in to my Grandmother's, I was very disconcerted to see Grandma start crying. Foolishly I had gone in uniform and the sight had reminded her of her youngest son, Frederick (my uncle) who had served

The author on embarkation leave, March 1952.

A Hastings of RAF Transport Command disembarking troops from 24th Infantry Brigade at Castel Idris Airport Tripoli in 1950 for Exercise "Quickstep". [Imperial War Museum]

throughout the First World War as a private with the 8th Battalion, Royal Warwickshire Regiment. He had somehow survived the trenches only to succumb to health problems soon after he returned home. Grandma had a large full length photograph of Frederick in uniform above her bed and had persuaded my mother to include Frederick in my Christian names in memory of him. I reassured her I was not going to a battlefront and Grandpa comforted her and stemmed her tears. During my leave I also went to "Jeromes", photographic studios in Birmingham to be photographed in battledress like hundreds before me. All too quickly the week passed and I went back to Beaconsfield to pick up all my kit, before travelling to RAF Lyneham where I met up with Johnny and Geoff. The army had recently started chartering civilian aircraft as well as using troopships and we boarded a Douglas DC3 Dakota in the green livery of Airwork. The Dakota was the first of several such planes I was to fly in during my service in the army and was truly a most wonderful aircraft – the

A Dakota C47 of RAF Transport Command, the military version of the Dakota DC3 in which I flew out to Tripoli. [Imperial War Museum]

workhorse of the skies. It was April and the weather was warm, almost too warm for our battledress uniforms. From Lyneham we flew to Nice, where we landed to refuel. I imagined all those wealthy holidaymakers lounging on the beach then after a break at the airport we flew on to Malta. We caught a glimpse of the Grand Harbour, Valetta – an impressive sight with British warships anchored in the port. British servicemen, together with men of the Royal Malta Artillery, were busy at Luqa airport where some troops disembarked for Malta postings. Then once more we were airborne and on the last lap of our flight to Libya in North Africa.

We eventually touched down at Castel Idris (named after the newly appointed King of Libya) which had formerly been known as Castel Benito, after the Italian dictator Mussolini. Castel Idris combined both civilian and service facilities and accordingly served both as an RAF station and as a staging post for civil airlines such as BOAC and Libyan Airways, the newly constituted airline of the Kingdom of Libya.

CHAPTER 3

68 AEC, TRIPOLI

As we disembarked from the Dakota, I felt the hot African sun on my back for the first time. We were met by a welcoming party of three. The first was a confident sunbronzed RAEC sergeant who had just come to the end of his National Service. The second was a young redheaded sergeant who, needless to say, was known to everyone as Ginger. The third was a strange foreign-looking fellow wearing Arab dress together with a pair of studded football boots although there was no sign of a sports field. The sergeant going home and waiting for his plane explained that Ayid (for that was the Arab's name) was a mess orderly at HQ Tripoli District. He had long coveted the football boots and they were a parting gift. Ayid was not likely to be playing however as he had very poor sight with just one eye, the other having been blind since childhood. We made our way to the Bedford truck awaiting us, complete with Italian driver. Ayid insisted on carrying all our kitbags, Ginger got in the front with the driver, we all jumped in the back and with no other formalities we left the airport and set off on the 20 mile journey to 68 Army Education Centre which was situated within HQ Tripoli District.

As we sped along in the brilliant sunshine, I had a feeling of excitement. I had survived basic training at Richmond and instructor training at Beaconsfield and had now completed almost a quarter of my National Service. I was still only 18 and already a sergeant in the British Army. With Local Overseas Allowance my pay was due to increase from 28 shillings (£1.40) per week to well over £8 per week, which was substantially more than I had been earning in civilian life. Now with everything found it would be possible to save some money, possibly even enough to buy a car when I eventually came out of the army the following year. I also intended to see as much as possible of North Africa whilst I had the chance. Even today Libya is a very difficult country to enter. In 1952 before overseas package holidays had become popular, it would have been virtually impossible to visit the country, except on military service.

We eventually arrived at HQ Tripoli District, a sprawling military complex of white buildings a mile from the town centre on the coast road, known to the locals as "Lungomare". The complex had formerly been an Italian Naval HQ and barracks. 68 Army Education Centre was a self-contained building within the complex with classrooms, offices and other services, including a fully fitted darkroom I was later to find useful when

The Lungomare, Tripoli: viewed from the old castle.

developing and printing the photographs I had taken. All Education matters in Tripolitania were the responsibility of Major Smithers whose HQ post was known as SO2 (Education). The Education Centre itself was run by a warrant officer who was a WO1 or RSM. Despite the fact that RAEC sergeants and warrant officers were usually seen as academic "schoolies", WO1 Ablett was a tall, rugged soldier looking more like a paratrooper than an army schoolmaster. We soon found we were being split up. Johnny Smaller was to be posted to an RASC Unit at Azizia Barracks where he would be instructing Drivers and other Service Corps personnel in

Main admin block, HQ Tripoli District.

basic academic skills, Geoff Barrett was to be posted to 9 Command Library in Tripoli town centre whilst continuing to live in HQ Sergeants' Mess. I was to join Ginger who was also an RAEC Sergeant. We would work at 68 AEC under WO1 Ablett training various classes mainly made up of private soldiers left behind in so-called "rear parties" whose regiments had recently moved on to Cyrenaica with the First Infantry Division (1 Inf Div).

Geoff Barrett sitting on the steps of the Sergeants' Mess, our new home.

My home for the next eighteen months or so was to be the Sergeants' Mess at HQ. I was surprised and pleased to hear I was to have my own room. It was a small room furnished with battered War Office furniture including bed, wardrobe, chest of drawers and chair, all of which seemed totally luxurious after five months in barrack rooms of twenty or more. In the corner of the room stood a washbasin and mirror. I soon found that Ayid, the orderly who had met me at the airport, was happy to keep the room clean, and arrange laundry and bed linen changes at the local *Dhobi* in return for a few piastres each week. Ayid was also always willing to help with blancoing and cleaning equipment and to all intents and purposes he acted like a batman to several of us, although of course sergeants were not officially entitled to such assistance. "Living in" sergeants and warrant officers ate breakfast and dinner (and sometimes lunch) together round a long table. There was an Italian chef, Angelo, and two Arab waiters and kitchen hands (Masud and Muftah), and we lived in some style. There was of course a Mess Bar run by a Scottish Corporal from The Gordon Highlanders, who acted as Mess Steward and was known as Jock. He always wore full Highland dress when on duty, including kilt and sporran. There were quite a few unofficial rules to take on board. Anyone wearing webbing belts or equipment into the Mess would be expected to buy drinks all round. Sleeves rolled up and shorts were to be worn to breakfast with a long-sleeved Khaki Drill bush shirt and long trousers after 6.00 p.m during the summer, and battledress with shirt and tie in the Winter. Father of the Mess was the HQ Regimental Sergeant Major, RSM Bright of The Loyals, who put up with the occasional youthful National Service sergeant foisted upon the Mess.

At long last, my own room in the Sergeants' Mess, HQ Tripoli District.

In addition to being new and inexperienced, I was also National Service and a "schoolie" and I suppose it was inevitable therefore that I would be tested in some way (I was after all still only eighteen years old). Not long after moving into my new room I went upstairs to bed after a convivial evening in the Mess. Because of the heat I had taken off most of the bed clothes and left just a sheet on the mattress and a sheet to cover me. I turned down the top sheet being ready for bed and nearly had a heart attack. There in the middle of my bed stood a large lizard, its tongue flicking out looking nervously about. I was just about to shriek "Look what's in my bed!" and rush out of the room when I heard a few muffled whispers in the corridor outside. With heart beating furiously, I stood there and wondered what to do next. The bed was close to the wall and at the foot of the bed was a large window, securely closed at present. I opened both casements wide, took the top sheet off completely then turned off the light. I could just see the lizard still motionless in the middle of the bed. There was a little light from outside coming in through the open window.

Suddenly the lizard made a move. It climbed up the wall, its feet adhering securely to the perpendicular surface, slowly it made its way to the window and the light, paused on the window cill then started to climb down the outside wall to the ground. I rammed shut the window and sat on the bed trembling. There was still some whispers in the corridor but I ignored them, left the door shut and finally got into bed. The next morning at breakfast one or two younger sergeants said "Did you sleep OK last night?". I feigned surprise. "Yes", I said, "is there any reason why I shouldn't have?". They retired baffled, the older sergeants smiled. I had passed the test. I was a member of the Mess.

I gradually came to know and respect the other senior NCO's. Most were career soldiers and specialists in their own fields, hence their posting to HQ. There were several Royal Signals Sergeants and WO's because every HQ has a large contingent of signallers dealing with codes, signals and messages. There were RASC Staff Sergeants and WO's dealing with Army Legal Services and of course RAMC medics. There was an RASC sergeant in charge of Motor Transport, a sergeant from the Army Physical Training Corps to supervise the PTI's in the district and other specialists including Ordnance, Engineers and REME NCO's. Other sergeants and WO's in transit also occasionally joined us. I soon realised I was the youngest in the Mess, and in fact I was the only one still in my teens. Most sergeants and warrant officers accepted National Service men on their merits but one or two, perhaps understandably, made it clear they resented young National Service men reaching the rank of sergeant so quickly when they had had to serve for many years to reach senior rank. There were two other WO1's in the Mess. One was from REME with overall responsibility for LAD and Heavy Workshops the other senior warrant officer in the Mess turned out to be another member of the RAEC. WO1 Ted Croft was the Command Librarian who ran the Command Library in Tripoli Town Centre. The library was open to all ranks of all services and the army allowed any British civilian working in Tripoli also to use the facilities.

We gradually settled into our new routine. As the weather became hotter it became very difficult to work non-stop throughout the day. None of the buildings had air-conditioning and we relied on electric fans to try to cool us, which were not always very successful. Teaching soldiers was not too difficult. I concentrated on Stage 1 and Stage 2 English classes and there would be about 15 or 20 in a class. Although I was nearly always younger than the men I was instructing, the sergeant's stripes worn by all instructors meant there was never any problem in keeping discipline. Most of the men coming to classes were from Regiments where NCO's ruled very strictly.

I was quite surprised to discover how little some of the Stage 1 soldier students knew. Most of them were National Service whose education for various reasons had been sadly neglected. Instead of teaching them English grammar I found myself teaching some of them to read and write. They were keen to learn and I tried to show them something useful so that they could write their own letters home and I also demonstrated the layout of formal letters so that, for example, they could apply in writing for leave. It was a question of showing them where the address should go, where to put the date and how to start and finish such a letter. I tried to interest them in reading by suggesting suitable books. The work was rewarding despite its basic nature. The Stage 2 students were of course more advanced which necessitated more lesson preparation and essay marking. Stage 2 students tended to be very competent Junior NCO's and regular soldiers who needed Army Certificates of Education to qualify for further promotion. Stage 3 students tended to be taken by WO1 Ablett as Stage 3 was the equivalent of 'O' Levels and most of the soldiers were senior NCO's or warrant officers.

After a few weeks, the staff sergeant who ran the Orderly Office and who rejoiced in the name of "Slim" Vale, because of his bulk, mentioned to us in the Mess that there would be the annual cross-country desert run coming up. Seeing us as "schoolies", he asked jocularly whether we would like to put in a team of three. What I did not know at the time was HQ had never put in a team of NCO's for any sporting activities. Most NCO's at HQ were older and had admin or academic type jobs. Cross country runs were the province of the physically energetic units in Tripolitania who fiercely clashed in any form of physical competition. They included the East Surreys, The Royal Marine Commandos, The Royal Military Police, The 4th/7th Royal Dragoon Guards and 16th/5th Lancers. Coming from a school where athletics were the norm and having recently completed Green Howards' training, I agreed straight away that we would make up a team which included Ginger and Geoff. We prepared ourselves as best we could then, when the day dawned we changed into gym kit, and "pumps", the fore-runners of trainers. We were stopped by the RSM who told us to wear ammunition boots with hosetops and puttees and khaki shorts and tops. He reminded us it was the edge of the desert where the run took place not English fields. The run was of course much harder than we had ever imagined because of the terrain and intense heat. Fortunately, no-one was stung by the scorpions we saw, but I was glad to be wearing stout boots, rather than flimsy canvas shoes. There were more than a dozen teams and we passed a large number of competitors who had raced away at the start. Most were dehydrated and gasping for breath but RAMC orderlies were on hand to help those failing to finish the run. We were quite pleased to come third as a team but disappointed not to win. We made our way back to HQ and showered. The next morning, the Orderly Sergeant told us we were wanted by the Camp Commandant. Was this good news or bad? It turned out to be good news. He was amazed we had mixed it with the Marines and East Surreys and even more pleased that we had come third. HQ never entered anything and it had been left to the "schoolies" to do the honours. He would take us to

The Uaddan Hotel, Tripoli.

The Uaddan Hotel and treat the three of us to a slap-up celebratory dinner. Seeing us look downcast, he said to me "What's the problem, Sergeant?". I explained that the Uaddan was the best hotel in town, Officers only and out of bounds to NCO's and OR's. "So it is", he said and paused, "have you all got civvies?", "Yes sir", we chorused. "Right", he said "You'll come in as my guests". And so it was, we had got off on the right foot with the Old Man and earned a first class meal into the bargain. This event highlighted the difference between training in the UK and military service overseas. It would have been inconceivable at Richmond or Beaconsfield for NCO's to sit down and have a meal with an officer at a social occasion.

CHAPTER 4

9 COMMAND LIBRARY

After several weeks I had settled into my new routine at the Army Education Centre. One night in the Sergeants' Mess, however, Geoff Barrett had a quiet word with me. His boss Ted Croft had mentioned they needed more help at the Command Library. Another two RAEC Sergeants were expected soon from the UK and they could back up Ginger at the Education Centre which was starting additional classes. It was too good an opportunity to miss. The library was situated in what had been the modern Italian quarter of central Tripoli. It would be a wonderful opportunity to work off the base and see more of the real Libya. After a few words with WO1 Croft, I found myself posted to the library by our Big White Chief, the Major. Like Geoff, I would still sleep and eat at HQ Tripoli Sergeants' Mess, but I would work each day in the library in down town Tripoli. Our course at Beaconsfield had briefly dealt with army libraries and the role of the RAEC sergeant but I knew very little about librarianship. Geoff however was of course a professional librarian in civvy street and so he instructed me in the mysteries of librarianship, including the Dewey Decimal System of cataloguing books and the need to record them in Accessioning Registers. Work also included requisitioning new books from the Army Education Central Book Depot (AECBD) in the UK, supplying the units in outlying parts of Libya and maintaining the Military Reference Section which was in constant use by officers seeking to graduate to Staff Officer appointments. Before promotion to senior military posts it was usually necessary for them to attend the army Staff College at Camberley. First however they had to show they were capable of benefiting from such a course, hence their interest in the Command Library. There was a large lending library of 10,000 books which was used both by British Servicemen and by civilian staff working in Libya. We also discovered in those pre-computer days a brilliant card index system logging details of every book and its location. Other Sections included Naval Intelligence charts and documents marked "Secret" and a large collection of Classical Music records, all carefully catalogued.

The library regularly received display material and glossy photographs of current events in Libya and the UK, which formed the basis of displays and exhibitions we mounted in the library. Resettlement information of jobs available in the UK for servicemen, both National Service and Regular, also came in which had to be circulated to units and displayed centrally. There was always great interest shown in these jobs by National Service men coming to the end of their service.

A small reading area offered mainly British newspapers and magazines, plus the only English language newspaper published in Tripoli, "The Sunday Ghibli", the publisher being an expatriate journalist by the name of Johnson. Ted Croft had

Interior of 9 Command Library, Tripoli.

a private office to mastermind everything. Geoff and I were supported by a Greek civilian, Mr Topsidacoulos, who of course we called Topsy. How he came to be in Libya we never discovered but he was a cultured urbane man with full security clearance to work with us from the FSS We had to do everything from unpacking heavy crates of books to stamping library books when the lending library opened in the evening.

The library itself was situated on the top floor of a building situated in a narrow street, the address being 5 Via Bergamo. The building had a ground floor occupied by an Arab guard or *gaffir* who also served as liftman and

Topsy.

general helper in the library. The first floor was occupied by the Field Security Section of the Intelligence Corps (FSS) whose job was to monitor local political feelings in the bazaars, to engage and security vet all local civilians, Italian and Arab, working for the British Army and to periodically test the security of British bases in Tripoli with particular reference to the security of signal and coding offices at HQ and elsewhere. The second floor contained 7 section SIB, the Special Investigation Branch of the Royal Military Police, which handled criminal investigations into crimes committed by servicemen or women in Tripoli and crimes committed against servicemen or women in the territory. Virtually all the people employed in the building were senior NCO's or officers, many working in civilian clothes most of the time. There were several corporals in FSS some of whom had very foreign sounding names and all having wide multi-lingual skills. Alongside 5

View of Via Bergamo taken from Command Library.

Via Bergamo was a bombsite which had been cleared and fenced with barbed wire to form a special car park for military vehicles at the building. It was guarded day and night by Arab *gaffirs* who controlled the only entrance and exit. The vehicles in the car park included some anonymous World War II jeeps and 15 cwt trucks used by FSS, and a few Landrovers and Standard Vanguard saloons used by SIB. One or two of the cars were painted black with Libyan civilian numberplates. We were also authorised to park our Bedford truck, which bore the legend 9 CMD LIB. The whole building had an air of mystery arising from the specialised units working there. As most of the building relied on the library for background information, research or recreational reading, I gradually came to know all the various NCO's and officers working in the building. Next to 5 Via Bergamo was an Italian *Latteria* or milk bar which constantly supplied everyone in the building with coffees, iced drinks and snacks. There was no air-conditioning and the top floor where we worked took the full force of the Libyan summer sun whilst the heat from the lower floors rose to make the library a very warm place to work in despite the electric fans we had been issued with.

ORDERLY SERGEANT

Back at HQ there were military duties to perform. Every now and then, the Camp Commandant would come up with some idea to keep us on our toes. Normally, senior NCO's would get up, have breakfast then move off to various locations to carry out their duties. For a considerable time, Part I Orders posted by "Slim" Vale instructed us to parade every morning at 0730hrs for inspection by the RSM. Fortunately, these parades eventually died a death leaving us to get on with our jobs. Guard duties were always the responsibility of a section guard posted to HQ from various armoured regiments including 4th/7th Royal Dragoon Guards, 14th/20th Kings Hussars, 16th/5th Lancers or 17th/21st Lancers. They were always incredibly smart, armed with pistols, and supervised by a sergeant from their own regiment, who lived with us at the Sergeants' Mess. A regular chore was Orderly Sergeant. The first time I took on this responsibility I was given three pages of Standing Orders by the RSM which seemed extremely comprehensive and rather daunting. They started in the early morning when the Orderly Sergeant was required to do Reveille and make sure all the barrack rooms, which housed the "other ranks" most of whom were signallers, were visited and inspected. During the day other chores included visiting the kitchens to see the Cook Sergeant, attending all meals and recording any complaints (there never were any serious comments). At night, guards were to be visited, Arab *gaffirs* inspected, defaulters paraded, perimeter walls and fences checked, the NAAFI building visited, inspected and closed and the Sergeants' Mess visited. As the RSM reigned supreme at the Sergeants' Mess, the idea of actually closing the bar when Warrant Officers were present and still drinking was of course inconceivable. Despite the apparent enormity of the job for a young teenage sergeant, I soon got used to it. The HQ RSM made sure that young National Service NCO's such as myself did a substantial number of Regimental duties and these took priority over work in the library. As the focus of attention, we always had to be exceptionally smart with starched KD uniforms, polished boots and red and black "Duty NCO" armband.

There was invariably a Duty Warrant Officer with whom the Orderly Sergeant worked closely. There was also (allegedly) an Orderly Officer appointed each day but in all the days I did Orderly Sergeant, I very rarely saw an Orderly Officer apart from a few perfunctory visits at meal times. Officers, in general, lived at the Officers' Mess and might as well have lived on another planet. In the real world, (apart from the Camp Commandant who was only a captain and really a type of adjutant) the RSM, warrant officers and sergeants ran HQ, being as usual the backbone of the British Army.

Orderly Sergeants always found there were some problems or unforeseen matters to deal with. One evening Geoff Barrett and I came back to HQ after evening duty in the town. There had been some function in our absence and a large marquee tent had been erected on the sand adjoining the main base but within the confines of the camp. Serving as a drinks tent it bore the legend NAAFI in huge letters across the top. The usual armoured regiment guards had been replaced by Red Cap Military Police for the evening, presumably because of the presence of top brass officers. The next morning, the tent had gone and it soon became apparent it had been spirited away by Arab thieves who had rolled up in what appeared to be an army truck, dismantled and loaded up the tent and then driven away past the Military Police. The usual guard commander sergeant was pleased that he was not involved, the orderly sergeant of the day was landed with immense paperwork and the Military Police were left with egg on their faces. The MP's Special Investigation Branch was hurriedly summoned and a week or so later the tent re-appeared. The SIB had driven into the desert in their Landrovers, scanned the horizons with field glasses and soon located the tent with its giant lettering newly pitched in the desert and already occupied by a group of Arabs who had allegedly purchased the "war surplus" tent from the thieves. Unfortunately for the new residents the army soon repossessed its property and the honour of the Military Police was (almost) restored.

My new experiences as Orderly Sergeant also gave me a few grey hairs. One morning I woke to find my alarm clock had not gone off and it was already turned six. I hurriedly dressed and went to the barrack rooms to make sure everyone was on the move and fortunately everyone had already long gone into breakfast and the barrack rooms were all empty and tidy. After breakfast they were paraded by their sergeant major for inspection. One signaller who was late after breakfast and late on parade was put on a charge by his CSM Appearing before the RSM he gave as his reason for being late the fact that the Orderly Sergeant had not called at his barrack room at Reveille. This did not prevent him from being put on jankers but it also ensured I was hauled up before the RSM, fortunately informally and not on a charge. So far I had had a good relationship with the RSM, now I saw his Regimental side. I explained that I had indeed been late visiting the barrack rooms but that all the signallers had been on time at the cookhouse and there had been no real reason for the signaller being late on parade. The RSM listened impassively but then gave me a stiff lecture on the need to take my regimental duties more seriously. There would be no official report but I would find myself allocated more regimental duties including Orderly Sergeant and I would be expected to fulfil them 100% in future. I left feeling relieved but I did indeed find my name on the Orderly Office noticeboard a few days later to act as Orderly Sergeant once again.

This time all went well and at about 2345hrs I was about to turn in when there was a sharp rap on my room door. I opened it to find WO1 Ted

Croft, who was Orderly Warrant Officer for the day. There were only 15 minutes of my duty left but Ted said, "Hurry up Brewin, get yourself properly dressed and we'll do a night-time inspection". I put back on full uniform, boots and armband and accompanied him. As usual he was very smart with WO's uniform, peaked cap and swagger stick. We checked all the usual buildings, visited the guard, and made sure the NAAFI building (known as the Pigeon Club) was closed, empty and locked. Then Ted said we would check the sandy area where the notorious NAAFI tent had once been pitched. On the sandy front there was a large steel building with locked steel doors for secure REME Stores. It was guarded at night by an Arab *gaffir* guard appointed by FSS. On the night we visited the Stores there was no sign of the guard in question. Ted tried the steel doors of the shed. They were unlocked, and he attempted to open the doors but they appeared to be obstructed. Together we leaned on the door which gradually opened forcing back an old bed on which, stretched out totally naked and fast asleep, was the missing Arab guard. Ted took his swagger stick and beat a thunderous tattoo on the steel doors leaving my ears ringing. The effect on the *gaffir* was electric and instantaneous. He leapt to his feet, jumping to attention, trying unsuccessfully to pin his ID Card to his naked chest shouting over and over again "Me no sleep, me no sleep". When we eventually left him we had to laugh on the way back and Ted Croft said, "Some guard he makes, fast asleep in bed and stark bollock naked". We filed our report in due course and turned in about 1.30 a.m. The next day we found the guard had been sacked by the Camp Commandant much to the chagrin of FSS from whom he had come highly recommended.

CHAPTER 5

LIFE IN TRIPOLI

TRANSPORT

RAEC transport consisted of an Austin PU light vehicle for the major, a 15 cwt truck with Italian driver (which had collected us from the airport) for the Education Centre and another Bedford 15 cwt truck, also with Italian driver, for use by the Command Library. All the vehicles were a light sandy colour rather than the dark green vehicles we had seen in the UK. Each bore army registration plates with the equivalent Arabic characters and numbers painted on the bumpers. They were all right hand drive but we drove on the right rather than the left which sometimes made overtaking difficult.

Each day after breakfast, the library truck would roll up outside the Sergeants' Mess, with the Italian driver, Dino Perisinotto. He was a stocky Italian with broad face and wavy black hair. *"Buon Giorno Sergente*

The library truck at The Sergeants' Mess, HQ Tripoli District.

Brewin, Come state?", he would say. Then Ted Croft would appear immaculate as always, Geoff and I would climb in the back and we would be driven along the Lungomare with the morning sun in the sky warming our backs. Dino, on some occasions would take just me into town if the others were involved on other duties and this would give me the chance to try to learn a little Italian. Initially Dino wanted to concentrate on trying to teach me obscene songs but, eventually, I persuaded him to explain more useful words and phrases. One of my abiding memories of those mornings is Dino driving along the Lungomare singing an alternative version of *"la donna e mobile"* in a fine tenor voice.

Dino only worked during the day but we often carried out duties in the evening and either Ted Croft had to drive us or we had to make our own way, usually by walking a mile or so into Tripoli town centre. Neither Geoff nor I had a driving licence but one day Ted Croft asked me if I would like to learn to drive which would give us the ability to use the truck on weekends or evenings when Dino was off duty. I was only too pleased to take him up on the idea and was surprised when he offered to teach me himself. I can still remember the thrill of taking the truck past the guard post onto the roads for the first time. The guards didn't give us a second look but driving opened a new door of opportunity for me. Learning to drive in Libya was somewhat different from going out in a little saloon with dual control on made up roads. For a start, none of the vehicles had syncromesh gear boxes which meant we had to double de-clutch on every gear change after matching the revs and there were no indicators on 15 cwt trucks which made the use of hand signals essential. These were easy to give as there was no glass in the windows of our trucks. Bedford QL's had a semaphore arm turning left signal on the nearside but no indicator on the offside as the driver was expected to use his right arm when turning. There were no ignition keys in our trucks so we had to immobilise them when leaving them by removing a vital component such as the rotor arm to prevent them from being stolen by Arabs. There were no brake lights on many of the trucks so we had to use the slowing down hand signal in traffic. What exactly Arab drivers, camel riders and donkey carts made of all these signals is of course a mystery, although service drivers would recognise them.

My own training course also included a session with the MT Sergeant who pointed out all key engine components and showed me how to start a truck engine with a starting handle when the battery was low. It was important to hold the handle in such a way that, if the engine kicked back, the handle would not break your wrist. We were also given some basic desert driving rules. If your truck gets stuck in the sand, you can often

22609182 Sgt. KAF Brewin, RAEC. Happiness is a Bedford truck and a tank full of petrol.

move it by letting out some air from the rear tyres. Bedford 15 cwt trucks were 4 x 2 or rear wheel drive. HQ's Bedford QL's were four wheel drive and more suitable for desert driving. The MT Sergeant explained we could sometimes clear a little sand in the fuel pipes by blowing into the petrol tank. If all else failed and you were stuck with a broken down vehicle, stay in it. NEVER LEAVE IT. Someone would soon be looking for you. However fit you were, the desert would always beat you if you tried to walk, and the truck would give you shade. If we were going to be out for more than an hour or two, we always carried bottled water. All these tips are as valid today as they were fifty years ago.

After about fifteen lessons Ted put me in for a test and I was delighted to pass the army test. The army driving licence plus pink form enabled me to obtain a UK driving licence when I returned home, without taking a further test in Britain. The truck was mainly Dino's responsibility. Every day the MT Sergeant at HQ would put on the MT Section blackboard a task to be carried out by Italian or service drivers. It might be "change engine oil" or "tighten and paint all wheel nuts" and this would be done whilst we were on duty. Periodically the truck would go to REME LAD workshops for a major service, but all the trucks were remarkably reliable and very rarely let us down, a testament to Bedford build quality, and the Army's service and maintenance schedules. Every time our truck was used, a book in the cab, known as the work ticket, had to be completed with details of journey, mileage, driver and reason for use. The "work ticket" system applied to all service vehicles.

A DESERT PROBLEM

One scorching day I had driven across the desert road to an army unit to deliver books and courses needed by the resident RAEC Sergeant. On the way back I was driving alone when the truck gradually coasted to a halt. I was concerned as that part of Libya is incredibly hot and in fact the highest ever recorded temperature in the world of 136°F was once recorded at El Azizia. I checked all the instruments and tried the starter to no avail. I looked under the bonnet but everything seemed in order.

Back in the cab I noticed the petrol gauge was still showing plenty of fuel. Could it be sand in the fuel pipes? It was a remote road and I had passed no vehicles since leaving the army unit I had been visiting. I got hotter as the heat built up. I checked the fuel tank itself, which was empty. Why then was the gauge still showing fuel? Was the gauge faulty? Dino was very particular in keeping the truck tanked up, as fuel pumps were virtually non-existent except at military bases and in one or two civilian garages in Tripoli town. Suddenly the penny dropped! There would be another long-range tank fitted. Crawling under the vehicle, I located the second tank, turned on the tap fitted to the tank, got back in the cab, tried the starter and to my great relief the engine spluttered into life. Good old Bedford! I did not make an issue of this problem when I finally got back to HQ. It would have produced no sympathy merely jokes about my incompetence but it was another survival lesson learned.

SWIMMING

Due to the intense heat in the summer we had most afternoons free and we would then start work again as the sun lost some of its heat, working through the evening till 9 or 10 p.m. As the base adjoined the sea, we would make our way each afternoon down to the rocks to swim in the blue waters of the Mediterranean. My swimming, which had been pretty poor when I joined the army, improved with the frequency of the beach visits. From somewhere we obtained underwater masks and we could then marvel at the sea creatures inhabiting the rocky coast. The rocks were of lava-like volcanic origin, sharp to the feet but soon we would all plunge into the sea from them. Usually there would be Slim Vale, Geoff, Ginger, WO1 Ted Croft and other senior NCO's splashing about. Ted Croft noticing I was not very confident when swimming on my back helped me to float and swim more strongly. All this swimming turned out to be most useful when the Camp Commandant decided to post orders saying all senior NCO's would be tested in a sea swimming trial. We would be required to swim out to a raft moored offshore and back again wearing denim uniforms but no boots. Looking at the platform which seemed a long way off, I said apprehensively to the RSM, "What happens, Sir, if I can't make it and drown?" "In that case Sarnt Brewin, I shall have to fail you", he replied solemnly. Fortunately, we all made it there and back.

Geoff Barrett and Slim Vale on their way back from a swim in the Med.

THE CAR

One day in the Mess, Ted Croft announced he was thinking of buying a car. Whilst this sounds a very normal idea, it caused a great deal of interest. There were very few civilian cars in Tripoli and no-one at Headquarters, not even senior officers, owned a car. The Major in charge of the SIB drove a black Standard Vanguard, it is true, with civilian plates, but this was a military vehicle intended to keep a low profile. The head of the British Legation based on the Lungomare had a splendid Bristol 401 saloon car in metallic blue, but there were very few British cars to be seen on the road, although there was a main Austin dealer in the town advertising A30's and A70's in the local *"Ghibli"* newspaper. Nearly all the other numerous Military and Airforce vehicles carried Military registration plates. The car Ted had chosen was a Hillman Minx and in due course it arrived at Tripoli Docks. Dino drove Ted to the harbourside to collect it and apparently disaster was narrowly avoided when Ted checked the engine for oil after the car had been craned off only to find there was no oil in the engine. In due course he rolled

1. *Staff Sergeant Jeff Jennings and WO1 Ted Croft brew up for an English cup of tea. 2. A wild and empty landscape at Garian. 3. The Garian Pass road. 4. A quizzical look from a camel with two passengers on the road to Garian. 5. Troglodyte Arab cave dwellers at Garian. 6. Ted Croft takes a closer look at The Lady of Garian, a mural map of the North African coast in the shape of a reclining woman.*

up to the Mess in it and it was the subject of much comment and admiration. A week or two later Ted decided to take a weekend run out in his new car. Jeff Jennings, (an RASC Staff Sergeant) Tommy (an MP sergeant) and myself made up the passengers and we had a most interesting trip up the *Jebel Nefusa* (The Black Mountain not far from Tripoli) then over dried up *Wadis* or water routes, over narrow desert tarmac roads, then off tarmac road visiting tiny settlements, which were frequently inhabited by Italian families cultivating olive groves or fields of Alfalfa grass. We occasionally passed giant pre-war Fiat trucks with long bonnets and high sided loads of produce but there was little motor traffic, the rarely seen other road users being camels, donkeys, or little rubber tyred carts pulled by donkeys or horses. On one occasion we stopped to chase a huge lizard which vanished into the rocks. On another stop at Garian we found troglodyte Arabs still living in a settlement of caves. We also discovered a cave where some former World War II soldier artist had painted a cave mural depicting the North African coastline in the form of a reclining woman. This of course generated much interest and ribald comment. As we drove deeper into Libya, the temperature rose and the Hillman was in urgent need of water for the radiator. Fortunately, we found a lonely police station far

7. *The police post at Bivid - Birchnem, where we topped up the car with water. 8. Ancient dwellings still inhabited on the road to Jefren. 9. A stop for photos on the Jefren Road.*

from any major settlements. The police were only too pleased to help and soon we were on our way again. We had brought drinking water, bread, tea and fruit from the Mess and we occasionally stopped to brew up and have a meal. We also managed to get some food at a tiny Italian run cafe/hotel far off the beaten track. It was certainly a trip to remember.

A day or two later came a personal catastrophe for me. Ted had asked me to get something from the Hillman and, as I grasped the nearside front door handle of his shiny new car, the entire handle came away in my hand. How do you tell your Sergeant Major in the army you have just wrecked his prize possession? As RAEC Staff we tended to stay a close-knit collection of WO's and Sergeants but there was still that rank divide and I always called both WO1 Ablett and WO1 Ted Croft, "Sir" although I was on Christian name terms with most of the other Sergeants and Staff Sergeants in the Mess. I stammered out the terrible news in the Mess causing great hilarity amongst the Sergeants gathered there at the bar. Ted took it extremely nonchalantly blaming a faulty die-casting rather than me. Within a few days new parts had been flown from the UK and they were duly expertly fitted by REME LAD with the help of the resident REME Sergeant, much to my relief.

MAP READING EXERCISE

Our daily routine was occasionally interrupted by special events. Orders announced one day there would be a Military exercise for Tripoli District Units. As RAEC staff, we would be involved as observers on a map reading section of the exercise. I would be accompanying WO1 Ablett in Dino's truck but as the hours involved would exceed Dino's working day I was

Left: Climbing the road to The Jebel Nefusa on a Map Reading exercise. Right: Author at a stop for lunch, photo by WO1 Ablett.

nominated driver. I was pleased to have the chance to get out of the town to see something of Libya and eventually we found our map reference for an RV was high up in the mountains along the coast towards the top of the *Jebel Nefusa*, and a wonderful observation point (OP). This involved a hair-raising drive along narrow roads running round the mountains until we reached our destination. WO1 Ablett was the observer and I was merely the driver. On the way back the notorious *Ghibli* desert wind was blowing which soon whipped up the sand obscuring the narrow tarmac strips which formed the road back to town making it difficult to keep on the road. Soon the truck filled up with sand. We had no goggles but sunglasses helped to shield our eyes from the sand, which whirled around like dense fog. Amazingly the World War II Bedford engine kept turning despite the sandblasting and at long last we made it back to HQ. I stripped off my sweat soaked uniform and stood in the shower, watching the sand fall into the shower stall and vanish eventually down the plug hole. We had certainly earned the local "OEA" beers we eventually ordered in the Mess.

SPORTS

One day on duty in the library, we were visited by Major Burcher the SIB Major who had his office on the floor below. He asked me if I was the sergeant who had been on the cross-country run and then asked me if I had played Rugger at school. I told him I had played at KES and then for one of the junior Old Edwardian teams. "Excellent", he said "I'm getting a team together from this building to take on the infantry and tank regiments on the coast". Before I could back out, I was roped in for a practice match on a coastal pitch near HQ. It had been very hot and the pitch turned out to be as hard as concrete. I thought it inevitable somebody would get seriously hurt with broken bones, but, fortunately, we all escaped breakages and were just battered and bruised. Even the Major could see it was not really a proposition to carry on, so the whole team was put on hold till we had had some rain. I was not too sorry when this team eventually failed to get off the ground, but at least I had made a few friends amongst the SIB.

THE GLASSHOUSE

Around this time I found myself in what is commonly known in the Army as "The Glasshouse" – an army prison. Fortunately I was not there as a prisoner but only as a visitor. The circumstances leading up to this were as follows: One evening in the Sergeants' Mess the RSM announced we had been challenged by the Sergeants' Mess of No. 69 Military Corrective Establishment, some 20 miles out of Tripoli, to a shooting competition. It was his intention to meet this challenge by selecting a suitable team of five. There were one or two obvious candidates, including the RSM himself, the Regimental Quarter Master Sergeant (a World War II veteran in the Grenadier Guards) and a long-serving Company Sergeant Major from the Royal Signals. A Staff Sergeant from the RASC volunteered, leaving one vacancy on the team. The RSM looked round the Mess and said "We should also have a younger member for the team, are you any good as a shot, Sarnt Brewin?" As it happened I was quite a good shot. Four years in the Cadets at a school with its own .22 rifle range, an 'A' Certificate and a 'First Class Shot' in the JTC plus Cadet camps and Green Howards training had kept me up to the mark. "I'm not bad, Sir and I'm willing to come along, to make up the numbers", I said. So a week or so later we made our way out of town in an Army bus with a few supporters from HQ. The MCE was no holiday camp. It was staffed by Staff Sergeants of the Military Provost Staff Corps who ran the place with an iron discipline. Most of the inmates spent their whole time cleaning and bulling up kit and polishing the prison itself. They appeared to sleep on wooden framed beds with little in the way of mattresses or bedding. I was shown around but saw no billiard tables or radios, although there was a gym and an exercise yard. Of course there was no television. A Staff Sergeant explained that the prisoners were glad to see visitors and there was no shortage of volunteers to help on the range, changing targets etc. It served to break up the monotony of their existence and made a welcome change. The match passed off with much good humour. Once I had zeroed in the sights of the rifle provided for me I put up a very respectable score and, at the end of the match, HQ had won much to the RSM's delight. We were entertained in the Sergeants' Mess attached to the prison, then made our way back to base by bus driven by a patient RASC driver who had been waiting for us throughout the evening. Other similar competitions followed but the "Glasshouse" remains my abiding memory of our rifle team.

SOCIAL OCCASIONS

Social life at HQ revolved around the Sergeants' Mess and the RSM decided to organise a social evening on a Saturday about every four weeks. Eddie Edwards, the Sergeant Cook from the Army Catering Corps always made a special effort to provide an extensive buffet, most of which he cooked himself rather than relying on Angelo, our Italian Mess Chef. Some of the

Sergeants from outlying Regiments would also attend. Several had wives in Tripoli and lived in Married Quarters in the town. These functions were the only ones when any women were present and of course we had to look our best. Whilst Regular NCO's had impressive Mess Kit, National Service Sergeants had to be content with Best Battledress in the Winter months or a freshly starched KD Tropical Uniform in the Summer. These functions were a good chance to meet other NCO's for a few drinks. There were always a few "turns" towards the end of the evening as we had to make our own entertainment. For example, Eddie, the Cook Sergeant would regale us with a series of Al Jolson songs, always finishing with "Climb upon my knee, Sonny Boy", before making his way to the bar for a few bottles of local "OEA" beer, which he always referred to as his "neckoil". Whilst I was always happy to turn up I was not a heavy drinker although it would have been very easy to become one, as all the drinks in the Mess bar were very reasonably priced.

One Saturday when I had finished an evening duty in Tripoli town centre, I was making my way back to HQ for a social evening in the Mess, when I passed the little cinema in the town run by The Army Kinema Corporation. The AKC obtained a very wide and eclectic range of films for British servicemen to watch. In addition to British comedies of the Ealing Studios variety, they showed continental films, some French and some Italian with subtitles. These were all grainy black and white films and most of them were gritty down to earth post war dramas from Italy. Italian film stars including Gina Lollobrigida, Sophia Loren, Silvana Pampanini, and Anna Magnani were of course particular favourites with the army audience because of their ample charms, most of which were displayed during the various films to cheers from the audience.

On the night in question, "The Seven Deadly Sins" was featured as "*Los Sette Peccatos Fatales*" with

Tripoli town centre a few weeks after independence.

Italian dubbing and English sub-titles. I particularly wanted to see this film and instead of going back to HQ for the Mess Function, I went to the pictures. It certainly beat "Al Jolson" but I was very late back in HQ and by the time I looked in at the Mess, things were coming to an end. The next morning before breakfast the Orderly Sergeant had a word. "You are wanted in the RSM's Office at 0800hrs sharp", he said. This was the time defaulters were paraded and I was worried. I duly turned up with a clean uniform and the Orderly Sergeant let me go in first. There were a few anxious looking squaddies waiting in the corridor to be marched in but I was spared that humiliation. I knocked the door and went in standing to attention in front of the RSM who was sitting at a desk. He left me at attention whilst I was questioned why I had not been present at the Mess Function the night before. I explained truthfully I had come off duty in the town and gone into the pictures. I apologised and said I had not realised it was a parade and I thought it would be OK if I came in later. The RSM listened impassively as always and then made his pronouncement. "You are an educated man, you should have known it would be discourteous to come in late when we had guests. You were missed, but you are still a very young sergeant with a lot to learn. You must give priority to our *esprit de corps*. In future, whether or not it is an official parade, you will attend all Mess functions on time and properly dressed. Do I make myself clear?". "Yes Sir", I managed to reply. "Dismiss" said the RSM. I had temporarily blotted my copybook but in general I had fitted in quite well with my membership of HQ's Cross Country Team and the Sergeants' Mess rifle shooting team. The next time I was in the bar the RSM bought me a drink and I knew the matter was closed as far as he was concerned. Needless to say, I never missed another Mess function during my service in Tripoli.

LETTERS FROM HOME

All letters received were very welcome. Mum wrote regularly with news from home and once I received a picture postcard of London from Dad (I have it still) just to let me know they were all thinking of me. This little message reminded me how lucky I had been to have a happy childhood with Mum, Dad and my sister Barbara. I also had a cousin Brian, who was the nearest thing to a brother I could have had. Brian's father had died when he was only four and Brian, with his mother (my Auntie Maud and godmother) had gone back to live with Grandma and Grandpa in the old house, which also served as a shop in Aston (incidentally the house in which I had been

Left: I-Corps trucks on an MI8 exercise on the German frontier with Russia, early 1952. Right: Corporal Brian Moody, Intelligence Corps.

born). Through our growing up years, I had seen Brian once or twice a week and Dad had always included Brian in our family outings and annual seaside holidays. Brian was five months older than me and had been called up accordingly a little earlier. With his grammar school background, he had been selected for The Intelligence Corps and was now a Corporal in MI8, a department not as well known as MI5 or MI6. MI8 was the division of the I-Corps which dealt in Codes and Cyphers. Brian was currently posted to BAOR in Munster where his unit patrolled the forests on the Russian border setting up temporary listening posts with their camouflaged trucks recording Russian coded troop movement messages, then sending them back via HQ to the UK for de-coding. Brian's letter with his stories of his service was accompanied by photos of a typical mobile listening unit surrounded by a motley collection of men in what can only be described as very informal uniform who turned out to be his MI8 pals at work.

One day I was pleased and surprised to receive a letter from Anja, who had had her letter to me at the last address known to her, forwarded to Tripoli. She was now in Finland working as an airline ground hostess and her letter enclosed a photograph of herself looking extremely glamorous in uniform and standing in the entrance of a tour bus. Her letter, as always, was mainly in English, concluding in French. I now had to settle in one evening and reply to all these letters. I also received a rather strange letter from an Uncle (Uncle Charlie was also my godfather) congratulating me on my article in ICI Witton's house magazine. This was news to me as I had not

Left: A very important structure, the Mess Tent erected in a forest clearing near Munster. Right: Signals trucks in use by MI8.

written nor seen such an article. It turned out that a letter I had sent to a colleague at ICI's Metal Division about life in Tripoli had been passed to the Editor who had added some photographs from Keystone Agency and some background information then run it in "The Metals Monitor'. This was the

first time anything I had ever written had appeared in print and in due course I received a copy of the magazine. ICI's magazine, when it arrived, reminded me of my friends and former colleagues back home. After leaving school with HSC in Modern Languages I had obtained a post in Export Ammunition Sales at ICI's giant Kynoch Works. The job had provided me with some invaluable business experience whilst I awaited call up for National Service. In its heyday, "Kynochs" as it was always known, stretched in a square almost one mile by one mile. Products on site included non-ferrous rolling mills, ammunition manufacture both sporting and military, production of such rare metals as beryllium and titanium and a whole range of products including "Lightning" Zip Fasteners, "Amal" carburettors and "Kynoch Press" printing. Transport included its own railway

Burning unwanted documents before the I-Corps move on. Uniform is not quite up to basic training standard.

system with its own steam locomotives, and motor vans which carried neither registration plates nor licences as they never left the vast Kynoch Works. I learned much about weaponry and ammunition whilst at Kynochs which had its own rifle range and remember helping with the annual stocktaking when I was amazed at the millions of rounds of ammunition of all types safely stored. Explosives were contained in isolated huts so that one accident would not trigger a monumental explosion which could destroy the whole works. We were each given a "Shooter's Yearbook" which contained a little verse describing the golden rule of shooting in the front of the book.

> "Never, never, let your gun
> Pointed be at anyone
> That it may unloaded be
> Matters not the least to me".

My time at the Works was mainly spent in preparing and checking export paperwork and invoices (which involved some use of my languages) to cover the export of the ammunition ordered. I was always pleased to hear occasionally from people with whom I had worked; which of course generated more letters to be sent home.

"M.O."

The weather was incredibly hot and I had now reached my nineteenth birthday. One day I suffered intense irritation in the groins and found I had an extensive rash at the top of each leg. What on earth could it be? I sincerely hoped it was not some horrendous tropical complaint. After a couple of days it was getting worse and eventually I told WO1. Croft that I was extremely worried about it. "Prickly Heat", he answered laconically, "Get yourself down to the MO and get it sorted". There was a small medical centre at HQ manned by RAMC orderlies under the watchful eye of a grizzled Scottish RAMC Captain who served as HQ's Medical Officer and who had a reputation for giving short shrift to anyone he considered to be malingering or "leadswinging". I made my way to the medical centre and was greeted by the RAMC Corporal on duty to whom I explained the problem. "I'm sure the MO will be most interested and able to give you some relief", he said. This comment did not seem to tie up with the MO's reputation but I knocked on the door labelled "Medical Officer" as instructed and went in. To my horror and shock there was no tough Scottish

MO but instead I found a QARANC lady Captain in a cool khaki uniform looking tanned and attractive. "I'm looking for the MO Ma-am", I stammered, "I am the duty MO", she said "What's the problem?". I started to explain there must have been some mistake and started to back towards the door but she interrupted me and said "For goodness sake man, let's have a look at you". It was a cool quiet office with blinds drawn against the sun and I was facing a very attractive girl only a few years older than me. Reluctantly I obeyed and undressed, hoping my body's possible natural reactions would not let me down as she examined me. She took one look at the rash and said "It's OK, it's only a heat rash. It's a form of tinea and you can cure it in a few days with a fungicide type cream. I'll give you a prescription and the Corporal outside will give you the necessary tube of it. Now get yourself dressed. You should be OK for duty tomorrow". I managed to get myself together and went out to see the grinning Medic Corporal. "I told you the MO would fix you up sarge", he said. After calling him various unprintable names for not warning me, I managed to get the appropriate tube from him which did indeed solve the problem very quickly.

RADIO

One day we received a visit at the library from two male staff from No.1. FBS, the Forces Broadcasting Services radio station, situated just outside Tripoli. The library had a good collection of records and they were checking to see if they could borrow some for a particular programme. They were accompanied by a very attractive girl newsreader who also wanted certain books for a programme which I was only too pleased to find for her. This meeting with her eventually led at her suggestion to me broadcasting on an inter unit quiz programme. Later I was involved with writing and delivering reviews of recent additions to the library, along with Geoff who was really the expert on such matters. These reviews involved more visits to FBS. Unfortunately, I found the newsreader was in great demand by young officers for various Officers' Mess functions and I soon realised as a mere sergeant I was not likely to be able to offer such glittering "dates".

BOOKS

There were two bookshops in Tripoli, one being "The English Bookshop", which was a popular place for civilians and United Nations staff to meet as it also boasted a little coffee shop behind the bookshop itself. The other bookshop stocked only books in Italian, mainly paperbacks. I bought a few

Italian paperbacks to try to improve the basic colloquial Italian I had picked up from Dino. I also found through the library archives that there was an old Arab bookbinder in the Old Town and managed to get some of my paperbacks rebound as cloth hardbacks. One day in the library offices, I found a box which still contained a few copies of a little paperback called "Ancient Tripolitania", which was an absolute gem. It contained a mass of information on Tripolitania from pre-historic times through to the Roman occupation two thousand years ago. I learned much of the historic sites, many of which were close to British Army units and I managed to fit in a few visits to them for photographs when visiting army units near Zavia, Homs, Garian, Leptis Magna and Sabratha. "Ancient Tripolitania" had been written by D.E.L. Haynes, who had been with the British Administration in the post war years.

BRIGADIER'S VISIT

Ted Croft advised us one morning that the Brigadier, the senior officer in the district, would be inspecting the library the next day. Like all good managers, he wanted to "walk his patch". We all duly presented ourselves in best uniforms and waited for his visit mid-morning. It was a small establishment for him to inspect. There was Major Smithers from HQ plus Ted Croft as the Command Librarian, Geoff Barrett who was Ted's assistant and senior librarian, myself as a sergeant instructor, Topsy our civilian clerk, Dino our driver and Ahmed our liftman-cum-gaffir, six in all plus the Major. The Brigadier duly arrived and to my surprise was extremely affable and civil. He chatted to us about our training and former civilian lives and moved along our line-up. He then turned to our Major and said "I understood your establishment was six at the Library and there seems to be seven here". We looked along the line and found that a seventh man had indeed appeared. He was the Arab waiter from the Italian *latteria* next door who had brought up our usual cold drinks, found the Brigadier in attendance and quietly joined the line standing to attention as smartly as anyone. The Major had no idea who he was but of course we recognised him immediately and it was left to Ted to explain the seventh man away. The Brigadier took it very well and we made sure he shared in the refreshments which had been brought up for us.

PHOTO TRIPS

Back at 68 Army Education Centre, the facilities included a darkroom and with WO1 Ablett's permission and the help of books on photography in the Command Library, I began to develop and print black and white photographs taken with a Kodak Reflex camera I had bought from Jena's, the best camera shop in Tripoli. The old town was a wonderful place to photograph with its castle, cannon, port and winding old streets, some now markets, others sheltering mysterious high-walled buildings which rumour had it had once been the harems of the old Deys of Tripoli during the time of the Barbary Corsairs. The arm badge for HQ Tripoli District staff was in fact a black Corsair Ship in silhouette on a blue sea against a white sky. In the Seventeenth Century the Corsairs had become the scourge of the Mediterranean cruising along the North African coast looking for merchant men to plunder. In many cases the crews of such foreign merchant men were taken captive by the Corsairs and held in Tripoli or at sea until a ransom could be paid for their release. One of the earliest recorded lotteries was held in England to allow money to be raised for the ransom of English sailors held captive in North Africa. Unfortunately so little money was raised that Constables in remote parishes would compel convicted criminals and vagrants to contribute towards the lottery. By all accounts, the odds in those days of winning were some 60,000 to 1 and very much better odds than today's National Lottery. Tripoli was also the scene many years later of a very early American military action when US Marines joined in an attack on the Corsairs to free imprisoned American sailors. Those who died are commemorated in a small Christian cemetery in Tripoli which I visited one day and their heroic deeds are remembered in the US Marine Hymn "From the Halls of Montezuma to the Shores of Tripoli, we will fight our Nation's battles on the Land and on the Sea". Eventually the Corsairs were subdued by punitive expeditions mounted by The Royal Navy, whose job was to prevent shelter being given to the Corsairs in Tripoli by threatening to bombard the old town to rubble unless the Corsairs were excluded from Tripoli's harbour, their favourite refuge.

A cannon at the Old Castle Tripoli, a haven for The Barbary Corsairs.

Left: The Forum, Leptis Magna. Right: The Arch of Marcus Aurelius, Tripoli, a 2000 year old marble lined arch.

The Roman ruins of Leptis Magna were also a magnificent sight and Tripoli town itself still featured the Arch of Marcus Aurelius beneath which the victorious legions of the Roman Army had once marched. In Sabratha along the coast from Tripoli stood a noble Roman amphitheatre and one

Roman columns in the sunshine at Sabratha.

magical evening in late summer the RAEC contingent from Tripoli, including Ted, Geoff, Ginger and myself made our way by truck to the 2000 year old open air theatre. With a darkening sky and a backdrop of blue Mediterranean Sea, the old Roman columns were floodlit into life for a concert of classical and opera music featuring a small orchestra and Nell Rankin, a Mezzosoprano from the Metropolitan Opera New York. Near the Roman ruins stood a British Army base, home to an armoured regiment. At the time of the concert the regiment was the 4th/7th Royal Dragoon Guards and the audience that night included many troopers from that regiment who, I have to say, behaved impeccably as if overawed by the unique occasion and the talent of the performers.

As the autumn approached, various changes in the RAEC establishment took place. We were joined by two new RAEC sergeants from the UK, Malcolm and Graham, who were also National Service and who were posted to 68 AEC to assist WO1 Ablett. Malcolm also helped out occasionally on evening duties with Geoff and myself in the library. After our duty had finished, we would make our way to a small café in the main square of the Italian quarter, drink coffee at an outside table and watch the world go by. We would then usually take a *gharry* or horse drawn open carriage clip-clopping back to HQ where we would pay off the driver at the barrack gates. Whilst the big hotels in Tripoli were out of bounds to NCO's and OR's, we all usually managed to find favourite eating houses, including a popular Italian establishment, not nearly posh enough to be called a restaurant, where the proprietor himself would serve us with heaped plates of *spaghetti-al-sugo*, a dish very akin to what is now called *spaghetti Bolognese*. Although the tables would fill up with squaddies from all the different units around Tripoli, I do not ever remember any fights breaking out although things would sometimes get a little boisterous as the evening progressed.

RAILWAY

One weekend I went into Tripoli town alone and found a little shop in a side street still selling pre-war maps of the town and its surrounds. The map proved invaluable in tracing the line of a railway laid by the Italians in pre-war years when the colonisation of the province was under way. I managed to locate the line which had been abandoned as World War II troops from Britain, Italy and Germany swept backwards and forwards across North Africa, I discovered an old tank engine rusting on a siding, some tank wagons which had apparently carried oil and a rake of wooden bodied

Left: An Italian built Railcar on Libyan Railways. Right: A tanker with tank wagons at Tripoli station.

coaches with open platforms at either end silently standing in the sun at an empty platform. The track, signalling and rolling stock had not been vandalised and everything stood waiting for someone to breathe life into the system once more. I measured the coaches and made drawings and photographs with some idea that the information might prove useful in the future either for an article or, more ambitiously, for a model, of the line.

The map which was in mint condition was packed with useful information as at 1934, its date of publication. To my surprise I found that the Officers' Mess at HQ had in fact been the original Governor's Residence and 5 Via Bergamo, site of the Command Library, had been the Provincial Headquarters of the Fascist Party of Italy. The period advertisements also conveyed a good impression of life in Tripoli in the 1930's when colonisation was still in full swing and Tripoli was a sophisticated Mediterranean city with Casino and Motor Racing circuit.

UNWELCOME VISITORS

A major problem in the Middle East is the devastation caused by locusts in the intense heat of summer. The British administration in Tripoli operated a Desert Locust Survey unit utilising British Army QL trucks to scout the Sahara and search them out. Locusts can do immense damage to crops in a very short time and forward warning and drastic attack on the insects is needed if swarms are to be avoided.

Another perennial problem was of course flies. To counter the risks to health posed by flies and mosquitoes the authorities would hang bunches of bay leaves on buildings at street corners. The idea was to attract flies and other insects such as mosquitoes to ensure their eggs were laid on the leaves which were collected and destroyed at frequent intervals before being replaced with more leaves.

A major scare which was totally new to me was the arrival of the bed bug. After several months without any sign of such activity I became aware of restless nights when I woke up scratching in the dark. Shortly after, Ayid came to collect the sheets for the Arab *dhobi* and showed me the tiny flecks of blood all over the sheets. "This is not good", he said, and I suddenly realised with horror what the problem was. I went down to the Quartermaster's Office and explained what I had seen and the army swung into action. First, I had to take all my clothes, uniforms and possessions out of the room, then two or three squaddies who worked for the Quartermaster Sergeant, arrived on the scene. My bedframe was taken away for minute examination and treatment, the mattress was taken away and burned, then the windows were shut tightly and a considerable number of DDT bomb-like canisters were fired all along the skirting boards and woodwork. The room filled up with a fog of insecticide, the door was shut and the room left to fumigate all day. That evening the windows were opened, a new bed and mattress were installed and very late at night, I moved back all my kit and gear. There was still a strong smell of insecticide about the room but it soon cleared with the windows wide open and that was the end of the bedbugs, thank goodness and thanks also to the prompt intervention of "Q", our Quartermaster Sergeant.

Changes now took place in the Mess. New arrivals were coming into the Mess from the UK including some War Office civilians on some mysterious tour of duty, which seemed to involve contact with LATAS or the Libyan American Technical Assistance Service, whose staff appeared on the streets in oversized, over-chromed four wheel drives carrying their own LATAS registration plates. The new arrivals forced a re-appraisal of accommodation and, after eight months in my own room which had a view over the Mediterranean, the RSM decreed I should move in with Geoff into a larger bedroom at the back of the Mess freeing up a room for one of the new arrivals. The new room looked down a narrow road which skirted HQ. The trees in the road harboured a colony of bats which zoomed around silently in the late evening. There was also a small mosque up which an elderly *muezzin* climbed laboriously several times a day to call the faithful to prayer without the assistance of loudspeakers or recordings now found in British Inner City Mosques.

WORKING YOUR TICKET

One evening in the Mess, we were talking about National Servicemen "working their ticket", the army term for obtaining release from National Service without completing the statutory two years' service. Various stories were recounted about recruits adopting eccentric behaviour in basic training in an effort to persuade their instructors they were mentally unstable and unable to cope with army life.

The MT Sergeant then spoke up to tell of his experiences with a young National Service soldier determined to get out of the army. The soldier in question had been called up into the Royal Artillery and carried out his basic training under continual protest. He had claimed he was exempt from National Service, his mother not being British. This having failed, he had tried to use United Nations statements to claim his human rights were being abused. He then claimed he had joined some obscure religious sect of which no-one had ever heard. All these arguments had merely earned him an exceedingly hard time with his instructors and endless "jankers" for misbehaviour. Eventually he had passed his basic training (probably because they were glad to see the back of him) and he had been posted abroad to a Field Artillery Regiment of twenty-five pounders based in Libya.

Here his protests continued and he soon obtained a reputation as a "barrackroom lawyer," the army term for someone who believes he understands Queen's Regulations better than his superiors. His actions became more eccentric and one day he cut off all his buttons as he said he should not be forced to wear the Royal Coat of Arms or the Artillery's badges. His CO had come to the conclusion he would be a serious liability in the event of the Regiment being called into action and came up with a brilliant idea. He would not recommend the soldier for discharge on mental grounds but instead he would have him transferred to HQ Tripoli District where he could do no harm. Arriving at HQ he was allocated to the MT Sergeant with whom he worked, continually complaining and maintaining he still intended to "work his ticket". The MT Sergeant explained to us he was in fact an intelligent man but that the whole business of National Service had taken over his life and he was obsessed with the need to escape from the army.

One day the MT Sergeant needed to send a Bedford 3 tonner to REME workshops for some major repair work and asked his new assistant, who had a driving licence, to take the truck into town. Unbeknown to the MT Sergeant, the reluctant recruit first loaded the truck with about forty jerrycans full of petrol then instead of driving to REME, took the truck into the old city into a narrow crowded street full of market stalls. Here he set up business selling off jerry cans full of petrol to willing Arab purchasers at a bargain rate. These goings-on attracted the attention of a Libyan traffic policeman on duty nearby and he in turn contacted the British Military Police on town patrol who arrived in time to catch the culprit in the act. The MT Sergeant spoke to the lad after his arrest by the Redcaps and discovered he was under the impression his latest masterstroke would finally secure his release. Instead, Army Legal Services at HQ felt the matter was so serious, it warranted a Court Martial. A defending officer was duly appointed who put forward all the arguments used by the recruit to obtain his release adding that working in extreme Libyan heat had probably tipped the balance and pushed the lad over the borders of sanity.

Unfortunately the Court rejected these representations, seeing the case only as theft and sentenced the culprit to two years imprisonment in a Military Corrective Establishment to be followed by a dishonourable discharge. Instead of a comparatively easy posting at HQ for his remaining service, he had managed to extend his military service from two years to three years and the rest of his time would be spent in a most unpleasant and strict environment. It was a sharp lesson to other National Servicemen who might be considering "working their ticket".

We fell silent after this cautionary tale and my mind went back to day one with Sergeant Kerridge at The Green Howards. The subject of the MT Sergeant's story had indeed chosen the hard way and found it extremely stony.

CHRISTMAS

With Christmas 1952 now approaching I received a very welcome parcel from home which contained amongst other things a large Christmas Pudding. The problem was how to heat it through thoroughly. Geoff and I tried unsuccessfully to warm it up in a basin over a paraffin stove sometimes used in the Mess when the weather turned cold. Eventually we had to give up and take it to Angelo in the kitchen of the Sergeants' Mess who was only too pleased to deal with it. Inevitably it was shared out in the Mess and I was lucky even to get a tiny portion of it. I was then able to write to Mum to tell her how much everyone had enjoyed it without revealing of course that I had first selfishly tried to hog it all with Geoff. When Christmas arrived, I realised it was my second Christmas in the army. Ted, Geoff and I celebrated Christmas Eve by lashing out on a dinner in an Italian restaurant in the town wearing civvies and hoping it was not an establishment reserved for officers only. Christmas Day lunch was of course served to OR's by sergeants and WO's from the Sergeants' Mess.

The weather was still warm and it seemed most unlike Christmas. Inevitably, I thought about my family back home celebrating in a traditional way and I knew they would be missing me.

About this time we were asked by our ultimate boss, the Major to help him with a move. He occupied an officer's flat in the town and he too had been moved to a different building by some obscure higher authority. I remember being told to pack his uniforms and when I opened the wardrobe doors I was taken aback by the range of clothes, including Service Dress with Sam Browne belt, battledress, fatigues and Mess kit complete with miniature medals plus civilian suits. In the 1950's British Army Officers always had to purchase most of their own uniforms from military tailors and I suspect the same applies today. Whilst basic military equipment was available to them, such items as Mess kit were expensive personal responsibilities. There were also items of personal furniture, books, china and glassware to be carefully handled. When all had been safely packed and moved in our RAEC trucks to his new flat, we left the Major and went for a celebration drink in a downtown bar.

We then received news that came as a considerable surprise to me. Geoff was promoted to Staff Sergeant, a rank not usually reached by National Servicemen. The purpose was so that he could understudy Ted Croft who was coming to the end of his tour of duty in Tripoli and who would shortly be returning to the UK. Geoff, as a Chartered Librarian, would be well placed to take over as Command Librarian with all the responsibilities currently borne by Ted who was a Warrant Officer Class One.

1952 had indeed been an eventful year for me. I had started the year as a private in basic training in the Green Howards in the UK and finished the year as an experienced Sergeant Instructor in the RAEC overseas. What I did not realise initially was that it was also a milestone year for Libya. Before my posting to Tripoli I knew virtually nothing about Libya but my travels by private car and army truck coupled with the books in the Command Library supplemented by talks with ordinary Italians and Arabs had given me a much better picture of the country. The Library was also sometimes visited by well educated Tripoli Arabs involved in Libyan Government Service from whom I picked up information on the political scene and news also came to me from British Army FSS NCO's who monitored the situation in the Old City.

CHAPTER 6

TRIPOLI'S HISTORY

In 1952 Libya consisted of three provinces, Tripolitania, Cyrenaica and The Fezzan. Tripolitania had a Roman background and Tripoli (known to the ancient world as OEA) had been its capital for 2000 years. Cyrenaica had developed under Greek influence and its capital was Benghazi. Tripoli and Benghazi had been nominated as joint capitals but Tripoli was much the bigger city and accordingly the largest centre of population in the country. Prior to the 1939 War the population of Libya had only been about 880,000. Now in 1952 it had reached 1,000,000 for the first time, still only the population equivalent to Birmingham's in a vast area of 1,800,000 square kilometres. Even today the population is still estimated at less than 6,000,000, despite an influx of oil industry workers. The Fezzan was a vast virtually empty province consisting almost entirely of Sahara Desert. During the 7th Century, Islam had spread throughout the whole of Libya replacing Christianity. In the 19th Century a very strong Muslim brotherhood was formed in Cyrenaica under the Senussi flag which gradually spread throughout Libya. Senussi towns based on the Muslim faith were set up in *zavias* or religious settlements. There was such a major settlement in Tripolitania which was also the home of a British regiment, the 16th/5th Lancers at the time I was in Libya. Whilst the Northern provinces of Tripolitania and Cyrenaica were predominantly Arab, The Fezzan was inhabited by a race of Negroid people similar to the populations of Chad and Niger which adjoined The Fezzan.

Early in the 20th Century, the Senussi had united with the Ottoman empire to thwart the return of Christianity throughout North Africa. In 1922 after World War I (which had finished in 1918) the Ottoman empire had crumbled

The Arab settlement and market at Zavia where a muslim school; established by the Senussi, educated the young.

and the head of the Senussi Brotherhood (Muhammad Idris) was exiled and had to leave the country. This left the way open to the Italians who had ambitions to develop an Italian empire in Africa similar to the British, French, Portuguese and Germans, all of whom had already established colonies and dominions in Africa. The Italians had originally invaded Libya in 1911 and brutally suppressed the Arabs. Tripoli town was occupied in 1912, when the Turks ceded Libya to Italy under The Treaty of Lausanne. A long drawn out campaign against the Arabs then ensued, various tribes holding out for many years. The Southernmost province of Libya, The Fezzan, was not subdued until 1930. In 1934 the Fascists, under Mussolini, commenced colonising the fertile coastal strip of Tripolitania in due course sending poorer emigrants from Southern Italy to establish olive groves and farms, on land much of which had never been previously claimed or cultivated by anyone. The Italian settlement scheme's managers in Tripoli set up farms, each with animals, plough, harrow and tools then Italy sent nine ships, each containing some 2000 settlers to Tripoli where they were directed to the fully equipped farms waiting for them. Dino's family had come over from Southern Italy with this scheme and of course they saw the

1. On a visit to Olivetti, an Italian colonial settlement, the author stands alongside the fountain square.
2. Olive groves under cultivation.
3. The Catholic church at Olivetti with RAEC trucks on the left.

61

Fascists as their saviours lifting them from abject poverty to a wonderful life on the Mediterranean with their own land and property.

World War II had seen much fighting backwards and forwards across North Africa and eventually the 8th Army (Desert Rats) under General Montgomery had triumphed over the Afrika Korps under Field Marshall Rommel at the battle of El Alamein. Even during my stay in Tripoli seven years after the ending of the Second World War, casualties were still occurring amongst desert Arabs treading on mines and amongst Arabs trying to salvage equipment from knocked out tanks in the desert and in so doing setting off munitions still on board the tanks.

The Senussi had backed and assisted the Allies during 1939 to 1945, and as a reward, Libya was created as a federated state by the United Nations in December 1951, only a few weeks before my arrival in Tripoli. The effect of this was to establish a Kingdom under King Idris with many changes to daily life in the territory. The British had previously run Tripolitania very much like a British colony as a British Administration until the United Nations had sorted out a settlement. There had been "MAL" or Military Administration Lira as a currency. This was now

The newly formed Libyan Police band marches past the little mosque opposite HQ.

replaced by Libyan Pounds, each having 100 piastres and one Libyan pound equalling one UK pound sterling. The British police were phased out. It was intended a new Libyan Police Force would be established. It was kitted out in British Army uniforms with a strange conical hat to finish off the uniform. A police band was formed, which occasionally marched past my window at the Mess. Traffic Policemen were very smart with white *képis* and neckguards to keep the fierce sun off their heads and white arm bands for traffic control. Most of the real policing on the streets was in fact carried out by a Provost Company of British Military Police with their distinctive Red Caps and British Army vehicles, mainly jeeps, landrovers and 15 cwt trucks, all bearing Military Police boards on their radiators.

Libya, like all emerging countries, also set up a national airline (Libyan Airways) which bought a few planes from British operators. They included Bristol air freighters similar to those used on English Channel services by Silver City Airways and Channel Air Bridge. Post, Telecommunications, Public Works and Engineering were gradually handed over to Libyan departments by the British. As always I marvelled at Britain's efficiency in providing key people to sort out the devastation caused by War. In the main, Tripoli town had escaped major war damage and was a most pleasant mixture of European and African cultures. It was now 1953 and the newly born government of Libya signed a 20 year treaty with Britain giving the UK authority to keep military bases there in exchange for foreign aid, much to the annoyance of France who had had their own plans for the country. Libya at this time also joined the Arab League. France which had administered The Fezzan until Libya's independence, now had to withdraw its administrators and the Foreign Legion troops who had been stationed there, leaving France with no presence in Libya.

King Idris was of course a Cyrenaican Muslim and I became aware of discontent amongst some Tripolitanian government officials in the new administration. One gave me a book, in English, setting out details of the new Libya. There was also occasionally some unrest on the streets, mainly in the Arab quarter, but once in the streets outside the library. The FSS monitored the situation and one Intelligence Corps sergeant apparently always carried a 9mm Luger in a shoulder holster when visiting the old city. This may have been bravado as none of us ever carried side arms in the town and we never felt threatened in the old city. The only troops who permanently carried pistols were the duty guards on the gates at HQ and occasionally the Military Police when they were on protection duties when senior officers or VIP's visited HQ. All this background had gradually become known to me during my first eight or nine months and I now faced almost another year in the Army as my demobilisation was not due until November, 1953.

1953 was to become another momentous year for Libya when prospectors carrying out geological surveys, literally struck oil. The newly established Libyan government found itself rich beyond its wildest dreams and of course oil companies from around the World clamoured for concessions. Britain with its immense influence over the Libyans immediately secured a major concession for British Petroleum and other major concessions were eventually granted by Libya to American Oil Companies. The USA struggled to make its own influence felt in Libya and the following year (1954) after I had returned to the UK, the USA finally signed a formal treaty similar to Britain's, giving them rights to bases in Libya in exchange for American assistance (hence the Libyan American Technical Assistance vehicles I had seen on the roads).

In 1953, for the first time, a new radio station was heard on our radio sets at HQ. This was AFRS and in the morning we could either listen to British FBS with the dulcet English tones of Joan, the girl I had met in the library and a style very much akin to the old BBC, or the Americans' gung-ho style which started the day with the cheery announcement "AFRS, Wheelus Field, Tripoli, serving American Forces in North Africa" usually following up with Country and Western or Rhythm and Blues numbers, and a weather forecast.

Sometime later, a young Libyan was to join the newly formed Libyan Army as a junior officer. Sixteen years later Muhammat Gaddafi had become a Colonel and, as the focus of the discontent in Tripoli, masterminded a military coup in September 1969 to set up a new regime (which continues to this day) based on Islam, "Freedom, Socialism and Unity".

CHAPTER 7

BMH

1953 also brought a setback in health for me. I had been running a high temperature and one evening in the Mess I felt myself "blacking out". I can just remember some older sergeants saying "Has he been drinking too much?", and Ted saying, "Not very likely", before I blacked out. I believe the next thing that happened was that Ted organised transport to the Military Hospital outside Tripoli, probably using HQ Medical Centre's Army Ambulance, and I woke up the next day in a strange bed. The previous night I had been wearing battledress in the Mess, now I had no idea where I was and I was just wearing a pair of "jungle greens". "He's coming round", I heard a voice say and then two army nurses in the red and grey uniforms of Queen Alexandra's Royal Army Nursing Corps were looking down at me. "Where am I", I said. "BMH", replied the first nurse. "Why am I here?", I asked. "You blacked out and they brought you up from HQ. This is an isolation ward because we thought at first you might have paratyphoid but Sister has had a look at your AB64 and your jabs are up-to-date". This reminded me about my uniform. "What's happened to my clothes?", I asked. "Don't worry, they're safe". "Did you undress me and put me to bed?", I said. "Yes" they said, "but you don't have to worry we've seen it all before" and with that I was left on my own as they went to tell Sister I was back in the land of the living.

For about four days I was kept in the isolation ward. No-one told me anything about my health problem but a Duty MO prescribed tablets and looked in from time to time with a serious face. I felt very ill and the only other visitor was the hospital padre, which I did not think was a very good sign. Fortunately I gradually recovered and was put into a general ward of about twenty beds, both medical and surgical. Reasons for being there for the other patients ranged from varicose vein operations to recovery from various accidents because the Army is a dangerous place even in peacetime. There a few bad fractures and limbs in plaster but fortunately no gunshot wounds. I soon discovered I was the senior (and youngest) rank in the ward, the others being corporals and privates.

Now I was well enough to be aware of Sister who, quite frankly, was pretty glamorous in her QARANC uniform, being tall and brunette. Being an officer she was of course senior to all of us and I think it is true that everyone both respected and lusted after her. Every morning she would go through the ward making sure everything was perfect before Matron, an even more awe-inspiring but less glamorous female, made her entrance. Everything had to be cleared off locker tops, all patients had to lie in bed with sheets and bedding tightly tucked in with mitred corners. The idea that there could be any dust or dirt anywhere was of course inconceivable. (NHS please note).

Matron would then sweep through the ward like a galleon in full sail, followed by Sister and the two or three nurses on duty. After this inspection we were allowed when well enough to get up. Instead of our own uniforms, we were issued with "hospital blues", a blue uniform with white shirt and red tie and allowed out in the sunshine in the grounds. This idyllic existence came to a halt for me after about three days in the general ward when Sister stopped by my bed "You are making such good progress Sergeant Brewin, I think you should help my nurses in future". This was a mixed blessing, I could chat up two or three friendly nurses but I had to fetch dinners from the kitchen and serve them to soldiers still bedridden with post-operative conditions or fractures. This invariably generated jokes about sergeants only serving food at Christmas (an Army tradition) and of course ribald jokes about my new dealings with the nurses. I remember one day leaving the Ward with a pretty blonde nurse followed by comments such as "Give her one for me Sarge". These all came to a halt when Sister put in an appearance.

Several of the patients were due for discharge from the hospital after about fourteen days and hatched a plot to involve Sister. A box was found to take into the gardens of the hospital one day and some incredibly large crawling insect was captured and put in the box. The next morning before Matron's visit, the box was left on the table in the middle of the ward which should have been totally clear and polished. As soon as Sister espied the box she made her way to the table and opened the box. The immense beetle immediately put in an appearance fell onto the floor and set off towards her. Sister screamed, jumped on a neighbouring chair hauling up her skirt very high to reveal shapely legs in black stockings, much to the delight of the patients lying in bed. Suddenly Matron appeared in the door and order was soon restored. The beetle and box were disposed of and things were soon back to normal. Sister, having shown her human side, was even more popular with the patients. I discovered later from one of the nurses that Sister had mistaken the beetle for a scorpion. The hospital was used to dealing with scorpion stings some of which had had very serious consequences, hence her alarm. Shortly after, I was pronounced fit for duty by the MO. I handed in my hospital blues and had my own uniform returned before being picked up by Dino. During my stay I had had a visit from Ted and Geoff who told me it was believed my illness had been caused by drinking an orange drink, in the town, which although labelled "Fanta" had probably been manufactured in some back street dive, rebottled in an old bottle and sold as a real "Fanta". This was apparently a problem both with fizzy orange drinks and with Cola bottles both being used for illegal bootleg versions. No-one at the hospital had ever explained what had caused the illness which had apparently been diagnosed as food poisoning. It had been very pleasant to have female company after my recovery and I was sorry to leave BMH (and Sister) to return to HQ.

Back at HQ, I was soon on duty as Orderly Sergeant once again. I had been learning some Arabic from Ahmed at the library although of course I could not read or write it. When checking the *gaffirs* at night, I greeted them in Arabic and asked them how they were "As Allah wishes it, *Shumbashi*", they would reply in Arabic. On this occasion they made some mint tea, ceremoniously transferred it into small glasses all of which had to be passed round three times when we sat down cross-legged on the sand to drink it before we went back to our posts. As always, I found if you tried to use the local language, even if you pronounced it badly or used a wrong word, a friendly reaction would immediately be generated.

I occasionally used to play a game of snooker in the Mess and sometimes played a Military Police sergeant called Tommy Thompson. Military Police usually had their own quarters and Mess as it was not Army policy for MP's to become too integrated with other units because of the nature of the job they had to do. Tommy was a gregarious chap however who liked to call in

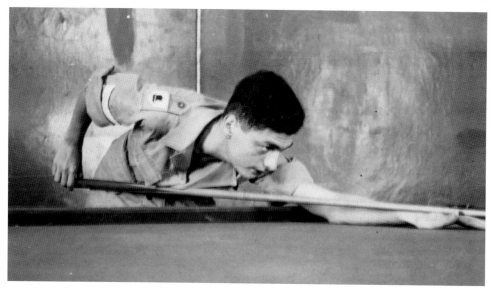

Snooker in the Sergeants Mess helped the author to relax.

HQ Mess for a drink when off duty and he was generally accepted as a member of the Mess. He was not however someone you would be likely to cross being big built with a fierce moustache. One Saturday, I had decided to go into Tripoli town centre. In the colonnade of shops in Tripoli's main street was the only high class jeweller in town. Ever since my epic sandstorm journey, the cheap Newmark watch I had bought myself when called up had been keeping poor time and frequently stopped. At the time I had bought it, I was only earning around £3 per week and the Newmark was the best I could afford. The sandstorm journey had also sandblasted scratches into my sunglasses and it was time to buy some new ones. I walked along the Lungomare in the sun and arrived at Climo's, the jewellers. The shop was fairly full with a number of prosperous Italians buying gold and silver jewellery. Eventually a young Italian assistant asked me if he could help (in a tone which suggested he didn't really want to) and I explained about sand in the watch and asked if it could be cleaned and checked. He said nothing but examined the watch for a few moments before tossing it back on to the counter. "This is a very cheap watch", he said "which would not be worth our time to clean and regulate". Before I could ask the price of a replacement watch, he had moved on to the next customer, a prosperous looking Italian in a smart suit holding up a gold bracelet he was thinking of buying. I felt very humiliated. I had walked all the way into town with the idea of buying some items from Climo's and I could not even find an assistant to show any interest in serving me. I went to my usual café on the corner of the main street opposite the Cathedral and had a coffee before taking a *gharry* back to HQ.

I was very subdued but Tommy the MP had dropped in to HQ for a game of snooker before going on duty. I was pleased to have something to take my mind off things and we settled down to a frame. He could see I was downcast and asked me what was troubling me. I told him all about the trip to Climo's and the reception I had had. "Were you in uniform?", he said. "No, I was just like this", I replied. He then told me to get changed and we would go into town. Outside the Mess stood his favourite WWII Jeep, suitably smartened up with white wheel nuts and Military Police sign boards. Waiting, too, was his faithful Corporal driver in Red Cap and white blanco. I reappeared in uniform, Tommy jumped in the driver's seat, the Corporal got into the back whilst I took up the passenger seat and we hurtled back into Tripoli.

We pulled up outside the shop, the Corporal took up station outside the shop in RP Order and Tommy and I went in. The little knot of customers gradually evaporated, a lady placed an expensive necklace back on the counter, a man replaced a gold watch and we were left alone in the shop with Climo and his snooty assistant. "Ah, Climo!", boomed Tommy "I would like you to meet Sarnt Brewin, my old mate and mucker. He is a big man up at HQ and also has an office here in town". Climo gave a sickly smile and shook hands with me. The snooty assistant had recognised me and was trying to fade into the background. "Sarnt Brewin here looked in earlier but you were too busy to serve him", said Tommy. "There must be some mistake", said Climo desperate to get rid of us as his shop stood empty and staring hard at the assistant now hiding in the corner. I explained about the watch and sunglasses and Climo soon came up with a watch which, although not exactly a Rolex, was shockproof, waterproof and sand proof at a very reasonable price. Soon I had also acquired a new pair of sunglasses, much superior to the battered sand scratched ones I had been wearing. I was about to leave when Tommy said "Are you sure there's nothing else you need Sarnt Brewin whilst Climo's shop is quiet?". I settled on a hand carved cameo which I thought I could take home for my mother and Climo, co-operation itself, offered me a special deal. I settled up and, to his great relief, we left the shop. I walked back to HQ leaving the MP's in town, but before doing so thanked Tommy for the moral support. He just growled, "Every now and then we have to remind them who won the f..... War". Years later, after my mother died, the cameo came back to my wife and was suitable redesigned as a brooch in a modern gold setting in Birmingham's Jewellery Quarter.

Life continued as normal at HQ. One day I was again on Orderly Sergeant duty sitting outside the Pigeon Club, the NAAFI mainly used by Corporals. Suddenly there was the sound of a motorbike and a sand and dust covered Don R roared up to me. The despatch rider in a leather jerkin, wearing crash helmet and goggles, dismounted and came over to me. What was happening now? Some crisis to be dealt with no doubt. But as the motorcyclist removed his goggles I saw to my amazement it was Johnny Smaller back from his RASC posting. Our SO2 Major had made some changes. Another newly arrived RAEC Sergeant was to take Johnny's place with the RASC and Johnny was to be posted to the Major's office as a sort of Office Manager. We went over to the Mess and sorted him out a room, then went to the bar to bring ourselves up to date with news as we had not seen each other for a few months. Soon the corridors in the Mess echoed to the sound of someone singing "I'll be Around" and voices could be heard groaning "Oh no, Smaller's back" and "pack it in Smaller". Johnny had landed on his feet. In addition to making Johnny his Office Manager, the Major had taken on an attractive Italian civilian secretary who was soon working very closely (some suspected too closely) with Johnny.

It was great to have Johnny back. With his laid back drawl he irritated and amused other older sergeants in the Mess in equal measure. Both being interested in photography we took cameras round the old city and developed and printed our photos at 68 AEC. Johnny had a very modern safari suit made for him by an Arab tailor we discovered in the old city. He proudly wore it to a Mess function but by the time the next function rolled round a month later, it had already began to fall apart, much to the amusement of the other sergeants. I had a pair of leather sandals made for me by an Arab shoemaker, which lasted much longer and in fact I wore them for several years after coming home.

A lonely gharry trots past Tripoli's Cathedral in the centre of the town.

Johnny now seemed to have acquired the RASC motor cycle on a permanent basis as I do not recall it ever being returned to Azizia. It joined our little fleet of RAEC vehicles although it still carried its RASC colours and was used by Johnny as his personal transport.

The Libyan Rope Trick. Three Arab lads with a rope climb a palm tree in the grounds of The Del Mehari Hotel in search of dates.

CHAPTER 8

TRIPOLI MUSIC CLUB

In Tripoli, life continued with the usual mixture of library work in the town and military duties at HQ. There were further changes in staffing. Ted Croft finally returned to the UK, his Libyan tour of duty completed. He had been a good boss to work for and had taught me to drive. I was sorry to see him go. Geoff Barrett was now promoted to WOII and appointed Command Librarian. Less than two years earlier Geoff had been a private in the Green Howards, now he was a Warrant Officer. Rumour had it that Ted was applying to be commissioned as an officer in the Royal Army Educational Corps but we never heard the outcome of this story. Geoff took his new rank very seriously and I tended to spend more time with Johnny Smaller, although I was still sharing a room with Geoff.

At the library, Geoff had come up with a brilliant idea. We could use the excellent collection of records we had inherited in the library to start a music club in the library. We called it simply 'The Tripoli Music Club', prepared posters for display in the library and selected an initial programme of music. We also used our friends at FBS to give a "plug" for our new music club in a radio broadcast. The day dawned and in the evening the Library closed as we prepared for the Music Club. People began arriving. We had been expecting servicemen but most of those coming seemed to be United Nations Staff, British Legation employees plus some officers and their wives. Geoff was organising the music whilst I took care of the administration, setting the room, finding enough chairs, handing out programmes etc. The music followed a similar plan for each meeting. An overture followed by a short piece of music, then an interval followed by the main work of the evening, usually a symphony. Geoff had researched the music with the help of FBS whilst I oiled the wheels and kept everyone happy. On the first evening all went well till the interval. Geoff and I were in uniform but virtually all the audience was in civvies. When we reached the interval a rather haughty young man, I took to be a subaltern in one of the armoured regiments came over. "Who is the officer in charge here?", he demanded. I explained there were no RAEC officers present. Geoff as a warrant officer was in charge. "My wife could do with a coffee, do you have any refreshments?", he said in the same tone a prefect at a boarding school might have said "cut along to the pavilion and get my cricket bat". We had no refreshments but Ahmed was hovering and I asked him to go to the *Latteria* next door and organise some coffees and cold drinks. Most of this conversation was in Arabic as Ahmed had taught me numbers one to ten and useful nouns and phrases we used every day. "Good God", said the young officer "you actually speak their language". This was said in an accusing rather than congratulatory tone. Ahmed soon reappeared with the young Arab from the *Latteria* who had joined our line-up when the Brigadier called. Everyone was pleased to see the coffee and soft drinks and left notes and coins which more than covered the cost, all of which I passed to Ahmed to sort out with the *Latteria* and the Arab waiter.

A more serious problem then cropped up. An elderly lady looking and sounding rather like the Queen Mother bore down on me. "Some wretched people were still talking when the music was playing. You must ensure total silence is observed during the second half of the programme", she pronounced. I looked round for advice but Geoff was busy with the sound equipment. Instead of making a general announcement I made an awful mistake. I knew the lady who had been talking, an attractive middle-aged woman who had obviously discovered a friend, not seen recently, at the concert. Seeing her standing alone, I said very quietly "I'm terribly sorry but someone has been complaining about people talking during the music. You and your friend would be most welcome to stay on for a chat when the concert is over". She coloured up very prettily and said "Oh goodness, Sergeant I hope I haven't been causing you trouble". "Not at all", I replied and at that Geoff announced the concert was resuming. I didn't mention the matter to Geoff but I vaguely regretted having spoken. The lady I had spoken to was obviously a much more pleasant person than the older woman who had complained.

The next morning, Geoff took various records and paperwork back to FBS, Topsy was out and I was left in charge. Suddenly Ahmed was tapping my door "*Shumbashi*, come quickly". I followed him out and we went over to the window and looked down into Via Bergamo which was a very narrow street. Below were two Libyan motorcycle police escorting a long black Cadillac which was followed by a further two police motorcyclists. A small flag fluttered on the car wing and I tried to see whether it was a Union Jack or a blue UN flag. It was obviously some VIP on a drive round Tripoli. The United Nations staff had taken over the Grand Hotel which was closed to the public. To my amazement, the cavalcade stopped outside our front door. "The Lift Ahmed", I said and Ahmed flew to the landing to take the lift down to meet our exalted visitor. I wondered whether he was visiting the Intelligence Corps or the SIB on the floors below then, with a sinking feeling, I heard the lift clang to a halt on our floor. I made my way to the office and sat behind the desk trying to look important. Ahmed knocked the door, opened it and said "You have a visitor, *Shumbashi*", and in came an imposing figure. He was tall, much older than me, wearing a smart linen suit and strangely, a black patch over one eye giving him a slightly sinister appearance.

"Do you know who was on duty here last night?" he said, without identifying himself. "Yes Sir", I replied, "I was". "I believe you found it necessary to take a lady to task for chatting", he said. "I'm sorry sir, but I am afraid I did in fact have a conversation with a lady but I hope I didn't exactly take her to task", I said.

He looked at me but said nothing.

Filling the unbearable silence, I went on "I do hope I haven't upset the lady in question Sir". Another pause and then he said, "As a matter of fact it was my wife". Oh No, I thought, this is not just an RSM matter, I am going to be up before the CO or reported to my Staff Officer Major. "I certainly didn't intend to create any sort of scene, Sir", then at long last he said "The fact is you were in a most difficult situation and by all accounts handled it very discreetly. My wife has asked me to pass on her apologies for putting you in such a spot. I hope she will still be welcome at future concerts". Relief flooded over me "Of course, Sir, I sincerely hope she will join us again". With that, he was gone. Ahmed took him down in the lift and I rushed to the window to see some minion open the door for him and then the little convoy swept off. Of course, I told Geoff all about it when he returned from FBS. He obviously thought I was making it up until Ahmed confirmed the whole incident had taken place. The lady in question did in fact come again, I am glad to say but of course I did not mention the incident to her.

CHAPTER 9

UK LEAVE

Back to normal library duties, we received a great many military reference books from the Central Book Depot in the UK. There seemed a preponderance of books on the American Civil War and on World War II. I read quite a few myself and found the book on Field Marshall Rommel by his son a particularly interesting book. It seemed to me it had been an equally matched battle between Rommel's Afrika Korps and Montgomery's Desert Rats. Visitors to the library included the Station Officer for BOAC from Castel Idris with whom I had talks about transport. He kindly brought me the papers to join the Institute of Transport but I felt I was too committed in the Army to take on anything else. There was also a young RAF Officer from the RAF Station at Castel Idris who was looking for certain reference books to help him pass Staff College exams for promotion. I asked Geoff to add these books to our next requisition and the Central Book Depot came up trumps by tracing and supplying the necessary books which we put on long loan to him. By this time we were all on christian name terms. "One day, I might be able to help you in return", he said when collecting his books. Other visitors to the library included some FSS corporals who seemed to have strange sounding Mid European names. After the War, the British Army recruited educated young linguists in Central Europe for MI9, another little known section of military intelligence. During the war MI9 had managed the escape routes for escaping POW's and aircrew who had been shot down. Later MI9 had been responsible for interrogating refugees to try to weed out Nazis hiding in their midst. Their job done, some NCO's stayed on in the Army and were transferred to FSS for field security duties. They were

Guns of the 42 Field Regiment, Royal Artillery visit Tripoli for Coronation Day celebrations. Note two different types of Quad gun tractors.

quiet anonymous NCO's and they wore no shoulder flashes on their uniforms to identify their regiment. In 1959, the remnants of MI9 were in fact integrated into 23 SAS (Volunteers).

Field Artillery guns on Coronation Day 2nd June 1953 parade.

It was now Spring 1953, Everest was climbed for the first time and news spread of the forthcoming Coronation of Queen Elizabeth II to be held at Westminster Abbey on June 2nd. Throughout the world celebrations would be mounted by the services and Libya was to be no exception. Plans were laid for a parade in Tripoli to be attended by detachments from all the regiments dotted along the coast. The day dawned, the sandy area around HQ had been cleared and a podium erected. Soon transport from infantry, armoured regiments and artillery rolled up at HQ and the parade assembled. As RAEC personnel, we were given other supporting duties which meant we did not have to join in the march past. This gave me the opportunity to photograph the parade which marched past the podium, the Brigadier taking the salute. As afternoon turned to evening, a spectacular firework display was set off by the RE's concluding with an EIIR in the sky. Car parks and MT depots were filled to capacity and sergeants from outlying units joined us in the Mess for an evening of celebration before all the various units returned to their remote Libyan outposts and HQ returned once more back to normal.

The RAF Officer for whom I had obtained special text books and course books turned up one day in the library bringing back all the books we had lent him. By now, despite the fact that he was an officer and I was only an NCO we were on very friendly terms. I was pleased to hear he had passed all his service exams and was shortly to be promoted. "I couldn't have done it without your help", he said. "I owe you a favour". I assured him it was my job to provide books and back-up to servicemen of all ranks but all he said was "I've got an idea and I'll be in touch" before he returned to the RAF Station at Castel Idris.

A week or two later, the phone went in the library office and it was my officer friend in the RAF, "It's all fixed", he said "We're flying supplies into Kenya over the next two weeks to help fight the Mau Mau and we'll be flying back to the UK later to pick up more stores. I've got permission for the plane to take you as a passenger back to the UK if you can square it with your boss and get some leave". I was overwhelmed. The idea of a visit to the UK had not even crossed my mind. I was relatively happy in Tripoli and due to return to the UK the following November. However, the more I thought about it, the more it appealed. I gratefully accepted subject to obtaining the necessary permissions and it was agreed I would phone Castel Idris if I could make it and I would then be told what the arrangements would be. My new boss was of course Geoff and he had no idea whether I could take leave or not. I had a word with Slim who worked out I probably had leave still due to me. I then had to fix up an interview with the Major with the help of Johnny Smaller. The Major seemed vaguely surprised but said he had no objection and he would give me the necessary written permission to leave Libya subject to my guaranteed return seven days later.

Playing snooker with Tommy, the MP sergeant, I told him my good news. "Lucky sod", he replied gloomily. "You remember my Corporal, the one who came with us to Climo's, he is desperate to get back to the UK He's married and his wife is very ill. The APM (Assistant Provost Marshall) has told him he can have compassionate leave but the Army won't provide transport and he can't afford the BOAC return fare". I paused between shots. "Do you think he could raise the money for a single fare if I managed to get him a lift with my RAF mate?". Tommy said "Do you really think you could fix it?". "I'll have a good try", I said. Of course my RAF contact was only too willing to help and so the following Saturday, Tommy rolled up with a Military Police Bedford 15 cwt and his corporal on board. We drove up to the airport and I said to Tommy curiously "What is this 40 mile return journey supposed to be on your work ticket?". "Town duties", he said with a grin. At the airport we reported to the RAF Station who were expecting us. An RAF loadmaster WO took us out to a Handley Page Hastings standing on the runway in RAF Transport Command colours. He settled us into extremely basic seating which had been lashed up for us. We sat with our backs to the wall of the loading area which was now empty except for a few ammunition boxes and the chains which had secured the arms, guns and ammunition they had just flown to Nairobi. Soon we were off on a perfect day and eventually we landed at Luqa Airport, Malta where an RAF Bowser tanker was waiting to refuel us. Our crew who had been flying for many hours needed a break and we were told to report early next morning before dawn. As a sergeant, I was offered the hospitality of the RAF Sergeants' Mess whilst my corporal fellow passenger was fixed up with a bed in an RAF billet. (Weeks later, I received a very modest bill in Tripoli from the RAF for my stay and the drinks in the Mess. I was only too pleased to pay it by return). Once again next morning

A Hastings of RAF Transport Command identical to the plane in which I flew home. The plane is on an exercise with the 16th Independent Parachute Brigade Group over North Africa. [Imperial War Museum]

we were airborne with the thunder of the four piston engines of the Hastings vibrating in our ears making conversation impossible. At long last we landed at RAF Lyneham in Wiltshire. We then split up, the corporal thanking me for fixing him up with such a brilliant lift whilst I, of course, told him I hoped his wife would make a good recovery (she did, I later found out from Tommy).

Then followed a long train journey back to the Midlands where my family were astonished and pleased in equal measure to see me back so unexpectedly. I was taller, fitter and much more sunburned than when they had last seen me I was told. The house, especially my bedroom, seemed very much smaller than I remembered it and I missed the heat and glare of North Africa's sun, to which I had become accustomed.

Going into my bedroom, I was surprised to see it completely clear and painted. I had always been interested in transport and I had collected "Bus and Coach" magazines for about two years. The huge range of consumer magazines now published did not exist in the Fifties and I had subscribed to "Bus and Coach", the industry magazine out of my very modest pay. Now they had all vanished, along with binders of notes I had built up on bus and coach fleets in the Midlands. I had also kept a file of "Modern Transport" newspapers and a scrapbook of Midland Transport articles. A neighbour of ours had garaged his car in our empty garage and I had discovered he was Works Manager at Mulliners coachworks in Birmingham. Seeing my interest he had kindly arranged for me to visit the works and had showed me round the workshops where I had seen coaches for Worthington Motor Tours, British Rail staff and the Army under construction. He had given me information on all these vehicles plus some back numbers of "Bus Transportation", the American equivalent of "Bus and Coach". All of these papers were also missing as were my books on the old LMS railway and my "war books" published by HMSO during the Second World War describing all the campaigns. Where could they be? I looked in the wardrobe, under the bed and on top of the wardrobe but there was no trace of them. All I could find was a small tin of black and white photographs I had taken of buses and coaches in various locations but everything else had vanished. I went downstairs to find Mum. "Do you like your room?" she asked brightly. "We've tidied it up and painted the woodwork". "It's fine" I said "but where are all my papers and books?". "Oh, we had to throw out some things but they were all out of date magazines and newspapers I thought you'd finished with". What on earth could I say? She had tried to make my home welcoming but I was very downcast. Unfortunately, worse was to come, I went down to the garage to take my bike for a ride but there was no bike there. This was a very serious matter for me. Cycling had been my favourite hobby and it was thanks to the bike I had been so fit when I went into the Green Howards with its demands on my physical stamina.

Mum and Dad had bought my first full size bike when I passed the City's eleven plus and had subsequently been offered a place at King Edward's School. It had been a Raleigh Sports in wartime black livery with black rimmed wheels and black handlebars. It had also been incredibly heavy with steel frame and steel mudguards making it hard work to ride. Four years later racing bikes had appeared in the shops in glorious metallic colours and lightweight frames. After saving every penny I could, I had raised the immense sum of £26.12.1p including Purchase Tax and had gone to the Heath Cycle Co to buy a Rudge Aeroclubman in polychromatic orange/red with lightweight frame in Reynolds 531 tubing. A new world opened up for me. Evenings would be spent "training" or speeding out to Coleshill with my friends. Gradually I improved the specification still further. I acquired a hand-built new rear wheel with fixed wheel for time trials with Kynoch CC. I read "Cycling" every week and bought other ultra light weight wheels with Simplex Derailleur gears like my heroes on the Tour de France. Our heroes of the day were Fausto Coppi, winner of the Tour De France in 1949 at his first attempt, and Reg Harris, professional rider for Raleigh Cycles, who broke the World Cycling speed record with a motorcycle pacing him at an amazing 100mph. I also bought a superior large capacity saddlebag for long distance touring with aluminium bag supports. In addition to the Bluemel lightweight mudguards, I bought lightweight short mudguards for sprinting through the Summer and the obligatory water bottles. I also fitted GB alloy brakes.

After a trial camping trip in Britain in Shropshire, I, along with two friends, had taken my faithful Rudge on an extended trip across France in the summer of 1951 a few weeks before call-up, crossing the Channel on a Bristol Freighter aircraft of Silver City Airways. We had wound up in Paris and had had a great holiday even though it included a night in a French police cell in Paris when accommodation and weather turned against us and a kindly gendarme took pity on us. Now the garage was empty, bike, wheels, accessories, spare high pressure tyres, saddlebags, everything had vanished. Again I went back to Mum and asked what had happened. "Mrs S had a word with me about bikes and I told her you had written to say you were saving for a car. I thought you had finished with the bike so I told her she could have it for her son". "Did they take everything?" I said. "Yes, they kindly cleared the garage for me". I bet they did, I thought. She went on "They did give me a few pounds and I put it into your Account of course". A FEW POUNDS, my heart sank. "I've saved all the money you have arranged to come from the Army pay unit. It's all there, I haven't taken anything out for housekeeping of course". Housekeeping! I had been abroad for well over a year, I had automatically expected all the money I had earned would be there. After all, my Dad had an excellent position as an Insurance Company District Superintendent. Mum's face looked worried. How could I tell her what I was feeling. "It's OK, Mum, I'll get a car when I come back", I said. "Thank Goodness", she said. "I just hoped I was doing the right thing".

Other lesser shocks came to light. I had cherished my 00 gauge railway and had built scratch models from plans bought with limited resources. All this had also been sold and the proceeds carefully placed in my bank account. "After all", said Mum "You're a man now. I knew you'd finished with all those models". I hadn't actually, but it was no use crying over spilt milk. Even my Scout equipment and the picture of Baden Powell, which had been hanging in my room before I went into the Army had vanished, given to a neighbour whose son had joined the Boy Scouts. I used to love visiting the Scout Shop in Dale End and had built up camping and uniform gear over the years. I had started with the 181st Birmingham (Sladefield) Wolf Cub Pack and had become a "Second" in my "six". Later I had joined the 70th Birmingham (KES) Scout Troop and had enjoyed camping in the New Forest with them. At least I still had my trusty clasp knife (I still have it) but it seemed my former life was being wiped clean in every way. I would have to start a new life when I returned.

Dad had sold the car during the War and was yet to buy a new one. I had a driving licence but no vehicle and even my bike had gone. I phoned my friends, including Philip Harber (another KES linguist) with whom I had toured France, he on his Carlton, me on my Rudge. Of course I had forgotten National Service. He had been a Sea Cadet and was now away in the Royal Navy. Other friends from school and from the Young Conservatives, to which I had belonged, were also away doing their National Service.

I phoned a girl I had known from King Edward's High School for Girls. Pat was a lovely girl with steady grey eyes, and she was also a very good musician with umpteen certificates hanging on the wall of her home. She was very pleased to hear from me and she was interested to hear all about the Tripoli Music Club. We went to the pictures a couple of times to see comedies starring "Bud Abbott and Lou Costello", which cheered me up. She had brains as well as good looks and helped me through the week which was not turning out as I had hoped. At Johnny Smaller's request I had been in to Birmingham to see a girl he had been going out with before his call up. She was working in a shop in the City centre. She seemed to have difficulty in even remembering Johnny and I privately thought that he would have to find a new girlfriend when he came back home. Dad had kindly offered to pay my fare back to Tripoli at the end of my leave and soon I was back on the train to London Airport, this time in civvies with my uniform packed away in a case.

I had flown home on a Service plane in uniform and no-one had even asked me for any identification. Now, I was in a civilian airport and found myself with an expired passport. Incredibly, in those more relaxed days, BOAC produced a passenger ticket card which was stamped at passport control after I produced AB64. Then we were aboard a Handley Page Hermes, a big comfortable piston engined aircraft which was in fact the civil aviation version of the RAF Hastings I had flown home in. Unlike today's occasionally offhand trolley dollies, BOAC stewardesses were very smart in uniforms very similar to the Services and nothing was too much trouble for them. Passengers who travelled in smart clothes expected a decent standard of service. Flying was still a minority form of transport enjoyed by a few.

I settled down in a quiet comfortable cabin with plenty of legroom, very different from the utilitarian and noisy interior of the Hastings. There was another passenger near me who turned out to be a friendly American businessman. During the seven hours flight we were served a very acceptable meal (with proper china and glassware) and chatted. He had been to London for a major project meeting and had taken the opportunity to have a suit made in Saville Row, and some shirts made in Jermyn Street. He was interested in National Service and asked me about my background. He gradually told me more about his own special project and it became apparent he was Vice President and project manager for the Wheelus Field Air Base construction project which was being built by a massive US consortium known as Crow Steers Shepherd. We stopped to refuel at Malta without leaving the plane and then it was on to Castel Idris where we landed in the early hours of the morning. He and I were the only passengers for Tripoli and we left the plane before it flew on further into Africa. I was very surprised to see an impressive Lincoln limousine with chauffeur waiting for my new found friend. The Lincoln was accompanied by a large American estate car containing a driver and another executive who had been sent to meet my friend who seemed to have a lot of luggage. It was now 2 o'clock in the morning and a BOAC duty officer appeared. Large doors were swung back on a Hangar type building and a BOAC coach appeared. Knowing something about coaches, I recognised it as a Harrington bodied Commer Avenger 35 seater in the blue livery of BOAC. My friend said "Surely they're not going to run a full-sized coach to Tripoli with just you on board". The duty officer confirmed this was indeed the case. "I have a better idea", said the American, "My friend can come with me and we can continue our most interesting conversation in the car". And so the coach was put back, luggage was loaded into the estate and we drove off into the night with our mini cavalcade.

After the twenty or so mile journey back to Tripoli, we sped along the Lungomare towards HQ. The Corporal in charge of the guard should of course have put the barrier down but instead, he turned out the guard who lined the entrance at attention whilst he saluted and we swept through the gates, the two long low American cars pulling up with a flourish outside the Officers' Mess. As a sergeant I was not of course entitled to a full turn out of the guard or a salute and I certainly did not live at the Officers' Mess. Our two cars had marker lights blinking, doors were slammed and my own very modest luggage was unloaded. My American friends got out of the car and chatted before saying goodbye and speeding off once more. I suddenly realised lights were going on in the Officers' Mess and I beat a hasty retreat to the Sergeants' Mess. Fortunately the main doors there were unlocked and I crept up to the room I shared with Geoff who did not stir as I crept into my bed.

At breakfast the next day the guard commander sergeant approached me "My Corporal tells me, he thinks it was you turning up with some high power Americans during the night. Was it you and what were you doing? Why were you at the Officers' Mess and who were they? What was their business here?" I was getting a bit fed up with all this questioning. This particular sergeant was another NCO with a chip on his shoulder about National Service sergeants. After all, I was a sergeant too. "I'm not allowed to discuss it", I said. This proved to be a brilliant move as it created an air of mystery which boosted what today would be called "Street-Cred", and caused considerable speculation in the Mess.

Initially, Wheelus Field flew WWII planes in the 1950's on missions in support of Allied troops in Korea. Much, much later I found that Wheelus Field was a staging post for the US Strategic Air Command and a bulwark against communism in the Cold War. SAC flew on three circuitous routes on a permanent basis and giant B52 Bombers, armed, as we now know, with nuclear weapons constantly circled the globe. One of the B52's was a flying command centre. Had the USSR ever attacked Europe or the USA with nuclear weapons, SAC would have reacted with unstoppable nuclear attacks on Moscow and other centres with devastating effect. This nuclear deterrent helped to keep the peace for fifty years until the USSR split into individual states, and the threat receded. Then at last NATO could relax and SAC could be stood down. B52's still form a terrible conventional bombing capacity in the US air force fifty years after they were conceived to keep the peace and have seen service as recently as the Iraq War in 2003.

As Wheelus Field was developed, American servicemen were confined to their huge base with its own shops, PX, and bus services. Air Police were occasionally seen on the street of Tripoli town in two colour American patrol cars complete with flashing beacons and sirens. They contrasted strangely with British Military Police service vehicles, which included WWII trucks and landrovers.

CHAPTER 10

BACK IN TRIPOLI

Back in Tripoli I thought back on my leave. Although it had not been an unqualified success, some things had turned out well and soon I received a letter from Pat, followed by a letter from Anja. Suddenly I was popular with the girls I knew. Whilst I had been away Geoff had organised a further Music Club Meeting in the library. Apparently, some well known music critic on his way to London from the Middle East had turned up and eventually a mention of the Club's activities had appeared in "The Times". Fame at last and I had missed the meeting, although at least I had the satisfaction of knowing I helped start the Club. A well known author, Nina Epton, had also come to the library researching her new book "Oasis Kingdom". I managed to get a copy in due course from The English Bookshop in Tripoli. I was glad to get back into the mainstream life of work at HQ and in the town.

One evening when walking back to HQ from the town, I passed a couple of vehicles parked on the Lungomare not far from HQ and thought I recognised them as I-Corps trucks from Via Bergamo. I thought no more about it. Later in the Mess, talk was of the increased security measures being put into place in Tripolitania. One reason was the construction of the Wheelus Field airbase, another was the unrest in the town following the establishment of Idris Senussi from Cyrenaica as King of Libya, including Tripolitania. "We could well expect an inspection visit", said one Signals Warrant Officer to another in the bar. At this, I mentioned I had just seen the Intelligence Corps vehicles on the road to HQ. The one Warrant Officer totally ignored me. I knew he did not have a lot of time for National Service sergeants and I was sure it was he who had reported me to the RSM the previous year and made a big issue of me being late doing Reveille. I moved away and a few minutes later, the other WO, a younger and more friendly type approached me. "Are you sure they were I-Corps trucks?", he said. "Our friend here thinks you are only National Service and how could you possible know anything about security", he went on. "He's wrong", I said "I know all the I-Corps trucks and staff because they share the same building with me and they were definitely FSS people".

At this he moved away and things began to happen. The Guard Commander was told to be exceptionally vigilant and to stop all incoming vehicles for an ID check. The Signals and Cypher departments were warned to make sure security systems were in place and the Orderly Warrant Officer and Orderly Sergeant prepared for a possible visit by checking the Arab *gaffirs*. Even the Duty Officer at the Officers' Mess was informed but what he did about it is anyone's guess.

An hour or two later, after lights out, the I-Corps did in fact arrive and had a tough job even getting into HQ. Everything was found to be in order and we were destined for a good report from Field Security but I felt a little guilty. My first loyalty was to my friends at HQ, but I knew most of the Field Security people through the library and realised they had a job to do.

A few weeks later there was an incident which caused me a lot of worry. It was the weekend, a Saturday, and Dino's day off. I took the library truck into town to pick up some papers and parked the vehicle correctly and in accordance with regulations in the Army compound adjoining the library building. The truck had been difficult to start and was in need of a new battery. We were obliged whenever we left a vehicle, even in an Army compound, to disable it by removing the rotor arm. However, I would only be in the library ten or fifteen minutes, the truck was virtually disabled anyway with a flat battery so I left it without doing so and went out of the car park. At the gateway, I asked the Arab guard to keep an eye on it and he smilingly agreed to do so. It took me a little longer than expected to sort out the papers I needed for HQ and when I reappeared about twenty minutes later, the Arab *gaffir* guards had changed and a new face greeted me at the car park entrance. To my horror, there was a gap in the row of trucks where my Bedford had been standing. I rushed back to the new Arab guard who seemed to have no idea what I was talking about. My Arabic knowledge was totally inadequate to deal with the problem, his English was virtually non-existent and I desperately tried in a mixture of English and Italian to find out when and by whom the truck had been taken.

Perhaps Arabs had stolen it, as they had been known to do in the past. Perhaps the previous Arab guard was in on it, hence his disappearance. Another thought struck me. Could Field Security have taken it having found out I had tipped off HQ about their raid? Whatever the reason, I would be in serious trouble for not immobilising the vehicle. Would there be a Court of Enquiry? I thought despondently or, worse, a Court Martial? I only had a few months left to serve in Tripoli and now this had to happen.

I made my way back to the main street whilst I tried to think out a plan of action. Coming slowly down the street was a Military Police town patrol in a 15 cwt Bedford similar to my missing vehicle. I would have to "bite the bullet" and report my truck stolen. I flagged down the vehicle and, to my surprise, I found the Corporal in charge was the very person for whom I had arranged a lift home. I told him my story and he then said, "Actually, Sarge, it was us who took your wagon. We tried every vehicle in the car park and yours was the only one not immobilised". "Where is it now?" I asked, "One of my lads has taken it up to the pound", he replied. The pound was an enclosure surrounded by high wire fencing where MP vehicles, damaged vehicles and confiscated vehicles were kept. "I could do with a bit of help on this one", I said and I knew he was thinking he owed me a favour. "Right", he said "Jump in and we'll go up to the pound. The Major's out at the moment and if it has not yet been booked in, we'll get it out again". I hastily jumped in and off we went to the pound where we just about caught up with the Lance-Corporal who had taken my truck there. He had not yet filled in any paperwork. What a relief. There was still a problem to overcome. The wretched truck would not start because of the flat battery. I was sweating anxiously and dreading the return of the MP's Major. After a time, the Corporal in charge called out about six MP's from their quarters and they unceremoniously trundled the truck, still with flat battery out of the pound and onto the road. There, with them pushing hard, the engine finally spluttered into life. I thanked the Corporal profusely and he was obviously relieved to see the back of me. I drove back to HQ and, on the Monday, gave Dino an almighty rollicking for letting the battery get into such a state. Needless to say, he was off immediately to REME, LAD who sorted the problem and a new battery was fitted the same day.

The whole episode was typical of Army life. Tommy had helped me sort out Climo, I had responded by fixing his Corporal up with a lift home. The Corporal in turn had got me off the hook by returning the truck from the pound without booking it in. Of course I told Tommy when he turned up at the Mess. "You were lucky", he said, "If the Major had been in you would have had it".

It was around this time that Castel Idris hit the news internationally. The RAF were aiming to break the World's air speed record with an ultra modern Supermarine Swift. The plains of Azizia in Northern Libya had recorded the

Mike Lithgow's "Swift" hurtles overhead with his recordbreaking flight on 25th September 1953.

highest temperature in the World (136°F on 13th September 1922) and the air above was accordingly thin offering minimal resistance to the Swift's sleek bodywork. Mike Lithgow as pilot went hurtling above at the appointed time and I managed to capture it on film as the Swift vanished across the desert, breaking the record as it went. For the record, Mike Lithgow's plane was a Supermarine Swift F. Mk 4 turbojet, the speed he reached was 735.70mph and the date was 25th September 1953.

CHAPTER 11

TUNISIA

My thoughts turned now to leave once more. Slim Vale, the ultra efficient supremo in HQ's Orderly Office, raised the subject with me. We had always got on pretty well although he had not been part of our little RAEC group, being a Staff Sergeant in the Oxfordshire and Buckinghamshire Light Infantry and extra regimentally employed (ERE in armyspeak) in Tripoli. He had the idea of a visit to Tunis in neighbouring Tunisia. He explained quite frankly that his languages were virtually non-existent and he thought the fact I had some French could be most useful. He was a quiet, smart NCO, much respected in the Mess and I was very pleased to be approached and immediately agreed to go with him. Arrangements then had to be made. First, I had to renew my passport at The British Legation on The Lungomare. Once again, Geoff Barrett agreed to my leave but explained that I would also need the Major's permission as my plans involved leaving the country. At an interview the necessary permission was forthcoming. There were one or two conditions. I would need to get the necessary Libyan Government approval to the appropriate foreign currency transaction and an exit and re-entry Visa. Only the *Banca Di Roma* in Tripoli could get the necessary authorisation. Because of the delicate political situation in Tunisia, we would need to go not in uniform but as civilian holidaymakers. The next stage was a visit to the *Banca Di Roma*, where I ran across a snag. The forms necessary for obtaining foreign exchange had to be completed in Arabic with English translation. Fortunately, Topsy in the library had the solution. He took our forms to an Arab scribe in the old city who filled in the forms for us in Arabic for a small fee.

At last the day dawned for our departure. Slim had obtained the RSM's permission for HQ's duty driver to run us up to the airport. We had booked single fares only to Tunis from Castel Idris and hoped to obtain accommodation on arrival. Slim had also obtained one or two hotel addresses from a contact who had visited Tunis recently and we intended to fix up a roof over our head when we reached our destination. The plane turned out to be a familiar Douglas Dakota DC3 resplendent in the refurbished livery of Tunis Air, a subsidiary of Air France. Boarding the plane in our civvies, we were surprised to find most of the plane taken up by French troops in *képis*, some wearing formal uniform others the baggy trousers of *legionnaires* from the Legion's Saharan Division. The common language they spoke was not, in fact,

French but German and I suddenly realised they were German members of the Foreign Legion. Their sunbronzed faces and confident manner made me guess they were all ex-Afrika Korps or ex-Waffen-SS, who had their own reasons for not wishing to go back to Europe. We eventually arrived in Tunis and went to the taxi rank. It was time to use my French. Slim had been given the name Hotel Transatlantique but the taxi driver did not know such a hotel. He thought perhaps we meant Hotel Atlantique so off we went to see the hotel in question. It turned out to be a palatial establishment on the Avenue Jules Ferrie with blue marble reception area. Slim took one look at the Tariff Board at Reception, picked up our bags and moved out on to the main street. "Far too dear", he said, "we would be broke in a couple of days". We moved lower down the street and found an impressive but smaller Hotel called The Carlton Hotel and booked in for our week's holiday. The prices were still high but just about manageable, if we went back to Tripoli by road instead of air. It turned out to be a good move for it was an excellent comfortable hotel. During the next few days we enjoyed the atmosphere of a sophisticated capital, similar in many ways to Paris but having markets and Arab quarters like Tripoli. We took the light tramway out to Carthage to inspect the impressive Roman ruins, visited the beaches which were almost totally empty in those pre-tourist days and sat at outdoor tables in smart cafes and restaurants relaxing

The cinema programme for our visit to the Palmarium, Tunis.

and of course watching French girls tripping by on high heels, as we sipped coffee and sometimes much stronger drinks. We also had one visit to the cinema. The building had a special feature in that the roof could be removed in hot weather and replaced when necessary. The Palmarium had been designed in the 1930's. (Cardiff's recently built football stadium is based on the same principle as is the proposed new roof at Wimbledon).

By and large we got by with my French despite a few blunders including the time I ordered for both of us in a French restaurant and asked for melon only to be served with an exotic fish dish. Slim asked me "What on earth did you order?". I discovered from the waiter he had

Mosque in the Old City, Tunis.

taken my pronunciation of *"melon"* to be *"merlan" (whiting)*, the fish speciality of the day. We bought the usual souvenirs from the Arab *souks* (including pottery and clothing we did not really need) and spent our evenings in the many bars to be found in the French quarter. We also managed to locate a French desert fort straight out of PC Wren. Rather unwisely perhaps, we entered the archway entrance which was somewhat incongruously adorned with a *Buvez Coca Cola* sign. Inside was hectic evidence of an imminent departure. Fierce looking French Colonial troops with faces covered against the sand were boarding battered World War II lorries, clutching ancient rifles. I took a few photos then realising we were vulnerable to accusations of spying, we beat a hasty retreat.

All too soon, the week flashed by and we realised we would need transport back to Tripoli. As expected, our funds did not run to air travel so we made our way to the bus terminus to check out available services. We discovered there was a trans-African service from Tunis to Tripoli running across the narrow tarmac strip which skirted and partly crossed the tip of The Sahara desert. It would be a lengthy two day journey with a stop at the Libyan frontier. We were asked for our passports and reasons for entering Libya. At this we had to explain we were British servicemen and also produced our AB64 ID documents. This was all noted and we were then finally sold the necessary tickets and told to come back the next morning.

That afternoon we had our last day on the beach. Suddenly Slim said, "Look at those girls". Further down the beach were two French girls sunbathing topless. In the 1950's this was a rarity and of course we decided to take a closer look. We casually strolled back down the beach, the girls apparently unaware of us. At the last minute they jumped up, raced into the sea, laughing and joking. We had to laugh too and Slim said "There's an army word for girls who do things like that", then we made our way back to the hotel to pack and pay our bill.

The next morning we soon discovered our coach standing alongside the coach station. It carried a large sign board on the roof with the legend "TRIPOLI", whilst a luggage carrying area occupied the rear of the roof together with two spare wheels. We boarded the coach which I noted was a French underfloor engined Chausson diesel and took our seats at the back of the coach on the instructions of one of the two drivers responsible for our journey. Gradually the coach filled up until there were no empty seats and the engine roared into life. Looking out of the window at our last look

The Chausson Diesel coach of Tunisienne Automobile Transports (which took us back to Tripoli) at the Libyan frontier.

at Tunis' suburbs, I became aware of a large amount of graffiti calling for liberation from France, the words being re-inforced by Communist Hammer and Sickle signs. France had invaded the country and colonised it in 1881 since when the country had always been administered by France. During World War II, the Afrika Korps had used Tunisia as a supply base to keep arms and ammunition flowing into Libya. This had been done with the help of a Vichy government. Before the War an Arab lawyer called Habib Bourguiba had put the case for an independent Tunisia resulting in his imprisonment by the French. After the War, Bourguiba had pressed the case for an independent Tunisia at the United Nations. In 1952, the year I had arrived in Libya, unrest had spread throughout Tunisia with demonstrations in the street, hence the warning from our Major to steer clear of political turmoil. Suddenly my thoughts were interrupted by the sound of a police siren, a jeep flashed past us signalling us to stop. This was the first of many unscheduled interruptions to our journey and we had not yet left Tunis. Armed French gendarmes mounted the coach, one with a complete list of passengers in his hand. They saw us at the back of the coach and came straight to us, the first one smiling and saluting. "You are

A broken down truck at Medenine in Tunisia causes problems for the Foreign Legion. Note the white képis and baggy trousers of the Saharan Division of the Legion.

the two British Military I think. May I see your papers", he said in English. We produced our AB64's which he inspected and gave back to us "You may remain here", he said. He then switched to French and everyone else was told to get off the coach. Grumbling, they all stood outside in the heat of the African sun. We sat in the coach with blinds drawn whilst the two drivers were told to unload the roof rack. Boxes, crates, cases and all manner of packages were then stacked at the roadside, carefully inspected by the police and laboriously reloaded before we were given the all clear. *"Bon Voyage"*, said the French gendarme cheerily poking his head round the door before allowing all the other passengers, mainly Arabs, back aboard. Of course there were many suspicious glances directed at us when the rest of the passengers finally reappeared. However, their attention was soon diverted. We seemed to have acquired an additional passenger after our stop. A very large elderly Arab lady in a long black dress and a collection of jangly gold coin necklaces had also boarded the coach. As there were no empty seats, she sat down in the gangway on the checkerplate floor. There was a heated altercation with the two drivers in French. "What's going on?", said Slim, I explained that it appeared she wanted a lift to the next village but had no money for the fare. After arguing for ten minutes, the coach at long last set off once more. We had been stationary for about an hour and now had a buckshee passenger. Soon an Arab village appeared and the fat lady laboriously dragged herself up and made her way to the door. The two drivers totally ignored her and the coach thundered through the village without stopping. She began to beat the driver about the head, the coach swerved across the road and then made its second unscheduled stop about half-a-mile past the village. She laboriously got off and we were eventually under way. Most of the Arabs thought the whole episode extremely funny but privately I felt very sorry for her, she seemed far too old and fat to be walking in that intense heat.

We had not studied the route before booking but a glance at the map of North Africa revealed the road to be taken. Leaving Tunis, the coach headed South to the coast road which ran through Hammamet and Kalaakebira to Sousse, a major city fronting the sea. Leaving Sousse, the coach headed inland to cut off the headland and wound its way to Sfax. The weather was hot, the sun was blinding and everyone had pulled down the blinds to keep the inside of the coach, which was not air conditioned, as cool as possible. The scenery changed from coastal to desert, but there was little traffic on the roads. Every now and then the driver would blast some inoffensive camel or donkey off the narrow tarmac strip which served as a road, by using powerful airhorns waking most of the passengers who were dozing. By late afternoon we had moved inland from Gabes once more and were driving along an empty desert road towards Medenine when misfortune struck.

There was an almighty bang and the coach slewed off the road, a second bump was felt and we came to a sudden stop. Fortunately no-one seemed hurt but first the drivers and eventually all the passengers climbed off the bus to stand in the intense heat to find out what had happened. Apparently a rear tyre had burst, probably because of the soaring temperature and the jarring impact on one side of the coach as it left the road with its full load of passengers and luggage had caused a second rear tyre to burst. We had not passed a vehicle for ages and I wondered how on earth we would sort out the problems. One of the French drivers soon took control. First, everyone had to stay off the coach, although there was no shade, except that thrown by the coach itself. Then the ritual of unloading all the luggage had to be carried out once more, with both drivers climbing the luggage ladder at the rear and pulling down all the miscellaneous sacks, cases, boxes and bags we had already seen when stopped in Tunis. Then doors at the back of the coach were opened as were side lockers and all manner of jacks and tools appeared. At this stage we noticed that the numbers standing outside the coach had multiplied. Arabs were appearing from the desert with fruit and bottled water which were snapped up by all the passengers. Slim and I had brought a few refreshments, including drinks, from the hotel but they had all long since been consumed on the coach and we were glad to buy the fruit and drinks offered, although I privately hoped they would not put me back in hospital. Slim later declared the Arabs had probably put nails on the road, and he may well have been right. The next stage was to unbolt and carefully lower the two roof-mounted giant spare wheels. Then it was a case of the drivers crawling under the stricken coach, where fortunately they found enough rocks and tarmac hardstanding on which to set the jacks. The men passengers, including Slim and myself, had been assisting with handling luggage, wheels and tools. Now we left the two drivers to swelter in the heat and struggle with the spare wheels. About an hour-and-a-half to two hours had passed when finally the two drivers felt the job had been safely completed and all luggage had once more been safely loaded.

It was going cooler as the desert sun moved towards the horizon. Soon it would go cold as the desert goes from one extreme to the other. At least, I thought, we could soon be on our way. I was in for a shock however. An announcement was made by the leading driver, first in Arabic then in French. "What's going on?", said Slim. I explained that as far as I could make out the drivers had decided it was not safe to continue. We must drive back to Gabes to the bus garage to pick up two new spare wheels and have the wheels and underside of the coach checked. This would add something like a further hundred miles to the journey, but of course it was a wise decision.

At last in the late evening we rolled into Gabes bus garage. The drivers announced we would be making an early start the next morning at 5.00 a.m to beat the desert heat and make up some time. We must all report to the garage early the next day. We were left to make our own sleeping or resting arrangements. Our luggage could be locked on the coach in the bus garage if we wished.

Slim and I found a little bar and joined some French ex-patriates at the bar. They were drinking yellow drinks smelling of aniseed which I discovered was pernod. We settled for beer and sat around talking for an hour or so. We still had a few hours before the coach was leaving but we had left most of our gear on the coach. In the end we rented a little upstairs room off the barman for a few francs. We snatched a couple of hours sleep fully dressed and at four o'clock made our way into the street where, amazingly, the same Frenchmen were still drinking at the bar as we went by.

Rejoining the coach, we set off once more with the same two drivers and headed south retracing our previous evening's journey, finally passing Medenine on the way to the Libyan frontier at Ben Gardane. Here there was another delay. Whilst Slim seemed to go through Customs and Immigration quickly, I found myself being interrogated by a hostile Arab frontier guard who examined my passport then told me that although I had permission to re-enter Libya, I had no permission to reside there. At this stage I thought I could pull rank. I explained I had permission from the Libyan Government because I was a sergeant in the British Army, I produced my Army ID papers, but he was not entirely convinced. He would allow me to enter Libya but Immigration had noted my passport number. There would be a requirement to report weekly to the Libyan Police Station in Tripoli. I protested to no avail, but when he stood up angrily and fingered his gun, it was time for me to agree and re-join Slim on the coach who, for some reason, found my predicament very funny.

We headed down the Libyan desert road to Tripoli on the last lap of our journey stopping at Zuara, then past the Roman ruins at Sabratha, scene of the concert I had attended the previous year. Passing through Zavia we rolled up at long last into Tripoli centre in our sand-stained motor coach. We gave the French drivers our last few francs, they had certainly earned it and we then made our way back to HQ where we could take a shower and catch up with some sleep. The postscript of course was the problem with the passport, but the inimitable Smaller in the Major's Office arranged for me to visit the British Legation where I was assured Immigration would have my "need to report" and passport number removed from the Libyan's black list. It had been a holiday to remember and I had found it fascinating to see some more of North Africa whilst I had the chance. The following year (1954) the situation in Tunisia deteriorated still further, and France fearing civil war, granted internal self-rule. Later still in 1956, France pulled out of Tunisia and in 1957 Tunisia became a Republic. All this of course was in the future.

CHAPTER 12

MALTA

It was now late Autumn and I would shortly be due to go back to the UK During my extended stay in Tripoli I had bought clothes, items for my room, books and presents for everyone back home. There was no way I could possibly get all this gear into my kit bag which would be bulging with uniforms and equipment. I mentioned the problem to Johnny Smaller. "Why don't you have a word with Jennings"? he said. "He has a reputation as a fixer". Jeff Jennings was a Staff Sergeant in the RASC and worked in one of the HQ Offices, all of which seemed to have strange titles. Jeff's boss was an Officer known as DADALS or Deputy Assistant Director of Army Legal Services.

Having put the problem to Jeff, he said "Leave it to me". The same evening two RASC squaddies turned up with a large white packing case on top of which were stencilled the magic letters MFO which I later found stood for Military Forwarding Organisation. I carefully packed all my goods and chattels into the box, excluding of course all my uniforms and military kit. Johnny then helped me to stencil my home address on the top of the box which we carried out to the entrance of the Sergeants' Mess. Passing by about half-an-hour later, the box had vanished. I had no idea whether it had been stolen or collected. It was in fact safely delivered to my home address to the surprise of my parents a few weeks later by an army lorry. I was never asked to fill in any paperwork for this box or to pay anything. It had just been quietly included in the next shipment from HQ to the UK. It was another example of it not being what you know in the Army but who you know.

I was beginning to think about returning to civvy street. I did not particularly want to go back to the same job at ICI Witton although I knew the job would be kept open for me. Details of various "resettlement" courses and jobs came to the library but none really appealed. I had become used to service life and wondered whether I should apply to join the Hong Kong police, who were recruiting Assistant Inspectors from the Army at the time. I also obtained some background information on careers within the United Nations which had some attractions because of the opportunities for further travel, together with the preferential rates of taxes which applied to such jobs. In the end I decided not to apply for any jobs in Tripoli but to wait until I had returned to the UK. Geoff, Johnny and I had joined up together and we were now notified by Slim we were in the same demob group. First we each had to see the Major who we had got to know over the last eighteen months. As always, we were each asked whether we would like to stay on but we had all decided we would opt to leave the Army. We were seen individually by the Major and thanked for our service. Our Army discharge papers ABIII were then prepared, each of course contained a reference. Mine showed conduct as "Very Good" and included the words "This soldier has shown a sense of responsibility beyond his years", which was not a bad postscript to my military service. We would be handed these papers when we eventually left the army after returning to the UK. Replacements for us had arrived a month or so before from the RAEC depot in the UK and we would be leaving them to carry out our duties. They were all Sergeants like Johnny and me and it was not clear who would take over as Command Librarian. Rumour had it an RAEC Officer from Cyrenaica, who had military library experience, would be brought in but we never met him.

A few weeks before our discharge date we were told we must report to Castel Idris airport a few days later for a flight to Malta. Now we had to say

British troops on guard duty at The Governor's palace, Valetta, Malta.

our Goodbyes to the people we had met and got to know, including the RSM, various Warrant Officers and Senior NCO's in the Mess, including of course Slim Vale, Tommy Thompson, the MP and Jeff Jennings. Time, too, to say farewell to Dino the Italian driver who had taught me some Italian and Ahmed who had taught me a smattering of Arabic. It was also time to say Goodbye to loyal Ayid who had looked after my room and kit so well for eighteen months. I passed over my remaining Libyan cash to him as a small gesture of thanks. Suddenly I realised how many friends and comrades I had made during my time in Africa, then it was time to pack our kitbags, vacate our rooms and head for the airport where once again we boarded a chartered Dakota, this time in Dan Air colours, for our flight to Malta It was quite a wrench to leave Tripoli which I had come to regard as my second home. Memories of the people I had met and the places I had visited would stay with me for the rest of my life.

Luqa airport was becoming quite familiar to me by now as it was my fourth visit in eighteen months. We were met by army transport which took us to Imtarfa Transit Barracks in the heart of the island. There were still some weeks to go to discharge from the Army and we were interviewed by the Transit Depot's RSM. Geoff being of course a Warrant Officer was immediately allocated a room to himself, Johnny and I were once again together sharing a room in the Sergeants' Mess.

The RSM asked me if I had had much experience as an Orderly Sergeant, to which of course I answered "Quite a bit at HQ Sir". "Good", he said "We're rather short of senior NCO's at the moment so I'll add you to the list. Keep an eye on Part I Orders and you'll be down to do a duty in a couple of days time".

Suddenly, we realised we were being left to our own devices and Johnny and I got a lift with some Royal Artillery transport into Valetta, Malta's capital, which we explored with our cameras, making the most of the Mediterranean autumn weather which was still warm and sunny.

Two days later I was indeed scheduled as Depot Orderly Sergeant and once again went through all the rigmarole of duties with the RSM. Finally the RSM said, "Don't forget to do defaulters at 1800hrs tonight. There are one or two troublemakers who keep showing up and two of them are on tonight. They have been told to parade in full FSMO (Field Service Marching Order). Check all their brasses (there would be 32 to be polished). Have you done any drilling"? I told him I had been an NCO in the Cadets for four years and would have no problem. "Right", said the RSM, "When you've finished inspecting them and marching them, double them around the parade ground a couple of times. Any Questions"? Almost before I could answer, he went on "Carry on" and I was left to cope in a new and very large base with sheets of duties to perform, which turned out to be very similar to the job in Tripoli.

All went well till the evening when I had to take defaulters. I made sure my own kit was up to scratch and went down to the Orderly Room. There were the two troublemakers, both of them Gunners in the Royal Artillery. They were fully kitted out as ordered by the RSM with webbing ammunition pouches, large pack, small pack, brace straps, water bottle and webbing belt, and I have to say everything was correctly blancoed with all 32 brasses gleaming. The RSM obviously had a very good grip on the base. There was however one almighty problem. I knew them both from back home!

Some years before, I had joined the Young Conservatives. We met regularly at Maitland Hall opposite Ward End Park and I was elected Treasurer of the branch. We periodically held dances at the hall and of course the reason why most young men had joined the Young Conservatives was to meet a number of attractive girls, who were aged between 16 and 24, who were also YC's. These girls formed part of my education by teaching me to play tennis and how to do ballroom dancing amongst other social skills.

The dances became very popular but they also attracted other young men whose purpose was to cause trouble. They came from tougher areas of Birmingham and by no stretch of imagination could they be classed as Conservatives. A more accurate description might have been lads who had had a few beers looking for girls and/or trouble. In the 1950's bouncers were unknown, but the men at the dance were occasionally called on to prevent known troublemakers coming into the dance. The two defaulters before me had turned up one night with another fellow and had been refused entry being pretty blotto at the time. As Treasurer I had been called over to the door because the two people on duty had been worried the takings might be snatched. The three lads trying to get in had been truculent. "Who's going to stop us coming in," they had said "Well, there's about fifty men in there", I replied "Do you want to take your chance"? At this they had roamed drunkenly away, threatening me with much effing and blinding. Now they stood before me at attention and of course they did not blink an eye, although I knew they recognised me from past arguments and altercations.

I resisted the temptation to hark back to our earlier meetings and simply went through all the routine I had been given by the RSM. By the time they had doubled round the parade ground a couple of times with all their kit they were absolutely shattered and I dismissed them. I could just imagine their comments when they got back to their barrack room!

Life is full of surprises, but I made a mental note to keep away from Maitland Hall for a time when I got back home.

The next morning the RSM had a word with me and the following conversation ensued.

"How did you get on yesterday, Sarnt Brewin"? he asked.
"Everything seemed to go according to plan, Sir".
"Any problems with the defaulters"?
"No Sir".
"What was their kit and turnout like"?
"OK Sir, they'd made a good effort".
"We might make soldiers of them yet. I'll put you down for one more Orderly Sergeant duty next week and then you'll be off".
"Yes Sir".

Of course I told Johnny Smaller all about it. "You're too bloody helpful" he said. "The RSM hasn't noticed me yet and you will have done two Orderly Sergeant duties by the time we leave. You need some relaxation". We moved on to the NAAFI. It was mid-morning and being senior NCO's in transit, no-one took much notice of us. The Sergeants' Mess bar would be closed and it was far too early in the day to start drinking anyway. We would settle for a cup of tea and a bun or a cake (a char and a wad in Army slang). There was a young girl of about 17 in the NAAFI, which was quiet, and she came over to chat to us. She was talking about the latest films on in Valetta and how she wanted to see the latest romantic comedy. To my amazement, Smaller kindly volunteered my services. "Sarnt Brewin here is a big film fan and he's off duty today, he'll be pleased to take you this afternoon". "Would you really", she said with big blue eyes searching my face. How could I refuse? Besides, she was a nice looking girl and I had nothing else to do. Arrangements were made and we walked back to the Mess. "You see how good I am to you", said Smaller, "I nearly offered to take her myself".

Later, we went into the Mess where lunch was being served. A grizzled BSM with the Royal Malta Artillery came over. "You're quick off the mark, lad", he said to me "Sorry, I'm not with you, Sir" I said. "Aren't you the sergeant who is taking Jenny to the pictures"? "Good grief", I thought, thinking the bush telegraph must be very good round here for people in the Mess to know already I was taking a NAAFI girl out. "Yes, that's right", I managed to say. "She has just told her father and he says its OK. He seemed to know you" said the BSM. "Are we talking about Jenny, the NAAFI girl"? I said uncertainly. "We are talking about Jenny", he said, "but she doesn't work in the NAAFI she's the RSM's daughter". "BLOODY HELL", I thought, "THE RSM's DAUGHTER. I will have to treat her with kid gloves or it will be me doing two circuits of the parade ground at the double in FSMO with a rifle over my head. Less than two weeks to go in Malta and another potential crisis. I will kill Smaller when I see him," I thought.

After lunch, I put on a clean shirt and my best uniform and went down to the entrance of the Sergeants' Mess, where I met Jenny looking very pretty and excited. Rather than cadge a lift in an Army truck and of course, it being the RSM's daughter, I had ordered a taxi by phone from the Orderly Room and off we went to Valetta in style. We did in fact have a lovely afternoon. She was very affectionate, cuddling up to me in the pictures and afterwards I took her to a little café for a meal after clip-clopping round the town in a horse drawn *carozzina*. Then back to Imtarfa in a taxi where I delivered her back safely to the married quarters where the RSM lived. It was with a mixture of relief and sadness that I left her. She was a very attractive girl and I had enjoyed our date. Gradually the spectre of the RSM had receded during the afternoon. Smaller of course thought the whole thing hilarious but swore blind he had not known Jenny was the RSM's daughter and eventually I believed him.

I did in fact do one more Orderly Sergeant's duty. It went off uneventfully and fortunately there were no defaulters to parade. The RSM was genial but made no mention of his daughter so neither did I.

Shortly after, our transit details came through. Geoff, Johnny and I were given details of our flight back to the UK. We said our farewells to new acquaintances, had our final big breakfast and went up to Luqa airport. Here we ran into a snag. Geoff being a Warrant Officer was ushered through but the Loadmaster in charge of departures told Johnny and me we could not travel. The plane was full and one officer had taken far too much excess baggage which meant we could not travel until the next day. Who was this officer who had caused us to delay our journey? I looked out on to the tarmac and saw a familiar figure strutting imperiously towards the plane. It was none other than the Matron of the British Military Hospital, Tripoli who had inspected me each morning as I lay rigidly in bed under tightly drawn sheets. She was a Major in the QARANC and apparently had accumulated a vast amount of baggage which now had to be ferried back home.

We had to make our way back to Imtarfa somewhat disconsolately to take various jokes and comments from the other sergeants who thought they had seen the back of us.

The next morning we were off once again to the airport. This time the whole plane was full of squaddies and corporals and Johnny and I were the only two sergeants. There were no officers or warrant officers travelling. One of you will have to be NCO i/c plane said the Loadmaster "Who is Senior"? "I am" said Smaller promptly. "Hang on a minute, Johnny" I said, "We were called up the same day and were made up to sergeant the same day. Why do you think you are the senior"? The Loadmaster was getting impatient. "If you were both made up on the same day, it comes down to your army number", he said. "I'm 22609186", said Johnny "and I'm 22609182", I said. "Right", said the Loadmaster "Sergeant Brewin is in charge of the plane". This sudden elevation gave me the need to fill in all sorts of forms for the stewardesses with whom I sat in the back to the annoyance of Johnny Smaller. Once again we had a chartered Dakota, this time from Airwork which took us back to Lyneham without any problems. My abiding memory of the flight was the sight of green fields through the window after months of sandy terrain. Back at Lyneham we ran into delays. Another lady was the cause of the trouble. Our plane's luggage would not be unloaded until a giant American airliner in US Airforce colours had first been attended to. Ground staff informed us the sole passenger except for U.S. secret servicemen was Mrs Eleanor Roosevelt, wife of the late US President. It took another twenty minutes or so for Mrs Roosevelt's mass of luggage to be cleared and a further half hour or so hanging about whilst she was cleared through the VIP Lounge. Then at long last we got our kitbags. Johnny and I had rail warrants to London where we were sent to yet another transit depot, the infamous Goodge Street Deep. This was a warren of rooms and offices deep underground adjoining the London Tube. Accommodation even for sergeants was very basic in dormitories with double-decker beds but the next morning, after a very decent breakfast, we finally made our way back to the RAEC Depot at Wilton Park, Beaconsfield, scene of our instructor course and my meetings with Anja all of which seemed so long ago.

Then it was paperwork to be completed in an office staffed by clerks who appeared to have no interest in the proceedings. Suddenly we found ourselves civilians in a world which had moved on during the two years taken from our lives. It was time to go home.

CHAPTER 13

TERRITORIAL ARMY

All National Servicemen serving with the army had a legal obligation to serve a minimum of three-and-a-half years with the Territorial Army or Emergency Reserve. The Territorials had traditionally consisted entirely of volunteers and this huge injection of young men joining the TA after completing two years full time service threatened to destroy the ethos of a purely voluntary organisation.

Not every serviceman received the same treatment. None of my friends who had been in the RAF or Navy were ever called for additional service. My cousin, who had been in the Intelligence Corps, was never called on to attend camps or evening and weekend parades. Unfortunately I found the army had not forgotten me. I had trained in the Green Howards whose depot was hundreds of miles up North and I had spent most of my time with the RAEC which had no TA Units.

Instead I received a notice telling me to report to 320 HAA Regiment (Heavy Anti Aircraft) which was based on the Territorial Army barracks at Washwood Heath, Birmingham. This Regiment was part of the Royal Artillery, a branch of the army I had not had much dealings with. I thought that it might not be too bad to go to TA parades on a part-time basis. The usual minimum requirement was six weekend attendances and an annual camp lasting fourteen days. Employers were obliged by law to release National Servicemen for such TA Camps and a small annual bounty was payable to those attending.

Unfortunately I was in for a nasty surprise when I reported to the Centre. I was told that my rank of sergeant during my full time service was "acting paid" only and lasted only whilst I was in the RAEC As I was now in the Royal Artillery I would have to revert to the substantive rank I had held before joining the RAEC which was that of a private in the Green Howards. The fact I had been in the Cadets as an NCO for four years, had held Certificate "A" as a Cadet, had qualified as a first class shot, had completed basic infantry training and had attended and passed a full time senior NCO's course was all to be disregarded. I had not previously served with the Royal Artillery and I must therefore start again as a Gunner.

As an experienced soldier with two years full time experience much of it overseas, I considered this unfair. I also found in conversations with other

RAEC sergeants posted to other TA Regiments that their experience had been welcomed and their rank of sergeant restored very quickly. Of course, National Servicemen who had served with local infantry, armoured or signals regiments were sent back to the TA Companies of their old regiments where they could meet up with former service friends. I knew absolutely no-one at the Royal Artillery Regiment. At first I attended a few weekend parades but I found that the officers and senior ranks were volunteers and National Servicemen tended to be looked upon as a necessary evil. It soon became apparent there was little chance of winning promotion. The gun crews too were either made up of volunteers or of men who had worked on similar guns during their National Service. Others, such as myself, would be found clerical jobs in the office or relegated to duties which were more like labouring than soldiering. In 1954 I was called up for annual camp on the East Coast and made my way by train with a warrant to join the Regiment at Weybourne, not far from Great Yarmouth. Here the gun crews would practise using drogue targets towed at a safe distance by RAF planes but still, I would have thought, a hazardous duty for the pilots of the planes towing the targets, bearing in mind many of the gunners were out of practice. Here, at last, I found a niche for my talents. All regular regiments and most TA units had a sergeant allocated to them from the Royal Army Pay Corps, but the Artillery Regiment I was serving with seemed to lack such an NCO. However, it was discovered I was a trainee accountant and so I was put to work sorting out the complicated pay and allowances earned by the servicemen at camp. I was given a desk in the Orderly Office and dealt with all manner of queries during the fortnight. Unlike genuine members of the Pay Corps, I was not restored to the rank of sergeant and so I supplied the services of a Pay Corps senior NCO for the pay and status of a Gunner.

Accommodation was basic in the extreme. We slept in old ridge type tents and used very primitive ablution and toilet facilities. Food was served in an ancient canteen and all in all, the facilities did not even come close to the infantry barracks, RAEC Depot or Headquarter accommodation I had had in the Regular Army. Off duty periods were highly valued and usually consisted of small groups going into Great Yarmouth where some of course got paralytic drunk, whilst others became involved in fights with soldiers from other units. It was not exactly the additional two weeks holiday some employers thought their Territorials were taking. It was a case, as always in the Army, of making a few friends from different walks of life, then making the best of it.

In the second year of my TA service, I attended even fewer evening or weekend parades. No-one seemed very bothered whether National

Servicemen got involved or not. I would have been very willing to get back into Army life part-time had the slightest encouragement been forthcoming, but it was not to be and I resigned myself to the fact that promotion prospects were non-existent. In 1955 I duly carried out annual camp, which was a re-run of the previous year at the same location with the same grotty facilities. Again, I occupied the Orderly Office and I dealt with general administrative matters, including queries on pay and allowances.

In 1956, I avoided camp entirely having moved to a new job where my services could not be spared. 1956 was also the time of Suez and of course I was still on the Army Emergency Reserve. Fortunately, although Royal Artillery Regiments were mobilised, my particular regiment being more concerned with UK defence than Field Artillery Service was not called upon.

My TA service was due to expire in May 1957 and I had a rare interview with an officer at Washwood Heath. I was asked if I would like to stay on with the Regiment in the TA. I explained that I felt my training and experience had been overlooked and I was still a Gunner after three-and-a-half years TA service. I also made it clear that I greatly respected the Royal Regiment of Artillery but that the way the TA was structured mixing

Three Gunners on the town at Great Yarmouth in 1954 (author on left).

Author and another Gunner, who shared the same tent at Weybourne, in shirt sleeve order in the sunshine in 1954.

volunteers and National Servicemen had seemed to lead to divisions in the Regiment. He took all this on board and asked me if I would consider staying on if a transfer to another unit could be arranged? I said I might be interested and to my surprise I was fixed up with an interview at another unit in Birmingham. I rolled up at the address given to me and found a large noticeboard "Special Air Service (TA)" with the winged dagger badge - "Who Dares Wins". In 1957, the existence of the SAS was hardly known to anyone and I assumed it was some sort of a branch of the Parachute Regiment. I was in civilian clothing and I was interviewed by someone I took to be the RSM who was also in civilian clothing. I explained my background and he seemed very interested in my infantry training, service in Libya, (The SAS had its roots in the Long Range Desert Group) rifle team experience and knowledge of languages. I did not know at the time that the SAS had a plan to re-organise into four-man teams, one member of which was intended to be someone who could pick up languages quickly. He could offer no immediate prospect of promotion, if I transferred it would be as a trooper. I would have to make a much more serious commitment to weekly training, I would be issued with a lot of expensive kit. It was May and the Regiment would be carrying out an exercise in Norway in the autumn, I must go away and decide whether I would like to proceed with my application to transfer from the Royal Artillery. The SAS was prepared to take me for training but I must guarantee commitment. I went away much heartened that someone had recognised my potential, the snag was the heavy weekly commitment the SAS demanded would clash with my professional studies. I was currently studying to become both a qualified accountant and a chartered Company Secretary. There was also talk at my employers of promoting me to a job elsewhere in the country at a different company within the group. This move did in fact materialise in due course. I talked it over with my girlfriend Julie, who was becoming a very important part of my life (she still is – we married in 1960). We had met at a Christmas Dance the previous Christmas Eve and I knew this time it was serious. After much agonising, I decided my long term civilian career must come first. I had served in uniform for a total of ten years as a cadet, full time National Serviceman and part-time Territorial, now it was time to concentrate on my studies for professional qualifications.

Reluctantly, I withdrew my application for a transfer from the Artillery to the SAS, went back to Washwood Heath, terminated my service with the TA, and handed in all my equipment and uniforms.

It was May 1957 and the end of my military career.

CHAPTER 14

RETROSPECT

One of the sad but inevitable results of growing older is that we lose touch with many of those people who were so important to us in our youth. People move on, change jobs and addresses, marry, divorce or go to live abroad. Despite all these interruptions there are a few loose ends from this narrative we can tie up.

Geoff – went back to librarianship in his native Yorkshire and contacted me many years later, although we have since lost touch again. He was the only National Serviceman I ever heard of to become a Warrant Officer.

Johnny – I kept in touch with for some time after we left the army, visiting him at his home in Birmingham and listening to his plans "to go into property" before losing touch with him again.

Anja – exchanged letters and sent me a beautifully illustrated book on Finland after I came out of the army before we eventually lost touch as we went our separate ways. I hope she found happiness in her native Finland.

Philip – with whom I toured France and who did his National Service in the Navy, made contact out of the blue from his home in Canada a year or two ago and we recently met after a gap of fifty years.

Brian – my cousin in the Intelligence Corps, sadly died two years ago after a distinguished career with the charity, Guide Dogs for the Blind.

Don – the bugler turned sergeant instructor at Beaconsfield, made an extremely successful career in insurance broking.

Barbara – my sister, lives in retirement in Rutland with her husband Barrie, another Old Edwardian from the Modern Language Sixth at KES and another ex-JTC member.

Julie – who was my girlfriend when my TA Service came to an end, married me in 1960 and we have been together ever since.

Savings – The savings account so carefully nurtured by my wonderful mother whilst I was away served to pay for my first car (an open red MG) when I came home.

The Green Howards – In November, 1997, my wife and I visited Richmond and went to the Regimental Depot which was just in the process of being turned into a housing development. The Officers' Mess had already been converted, as it stood, into two large dwellings, the Indoor Range we had scrubbed one night fortysix years earlier was now a Dance Studio, but the Guard Room, the Sergeants' Mess and the Barrack Blocks were still recognisable as was the barrack square which was just about to be built over. The Regimental Museum, scene of my visit on Boxing Day 1951, had been moved to Holy Trinity Church in the cobbled square in the centre of Richmond. We subsequently visited the museum which has been developed and expanded into one of the finest regimental museums in the country. Staff at the Museum gave us a guided tour and a warm welcome and brought back a few memories. The Green Howards as a Regiment still survives after 300 years of honourable service to the country and is currently based in Germany.

RAEC – The RAEC Depot at Beaconsfield, formerly the Army School of Education is now the Defence School of Languages specialising in training linguists for the Intelligence Corps. The RAEC itself was subsequently absorbed into the Adjutant General's Corps as the Educational and Training Services Branch of the Corps and is now all officer.

The Green Howards/RAEC Link – A year or two ago I discovered a link between the Green Howards and the RAEC, which may have accounted for my initial posting to the Green Howards for basic training before being sent on to Wilton Park for Instructor Training in the RAEC. In "Beyond Their Duty – Heroes of the Green Howards" by Roger Chapman, the story is told of Archie White, then a Captain in the Regiment who won the Victoria Cross for Gallantry during the First World War. Captain White was in fact the fourth member of the Green Howards to be awarded the V.C. during the Battle of The Somme.

After the first World War, Captain White took up a post as a Major in the newly formed Army Educational Corps which he joined in 1920. After a distinguished Army career including service in the second World War he retired as an Honorary Colonel in 1947. He was appointed Deputy Commandant of the RAEC 1960-1969 and in retirement wrote a definitive history of Army Education entitled "The Story of Army Education 1643-1963". He died in 1971.

The Royal Artillery – 320 HAA Regiment equipped with WWII 3.7 inch Anti-Aircraft Guns, during my TA service was subsequently converted into 443 LAA Regiment RA/TA with more modern weapons and continued to operate from Washwood Heath TA centre.

SAS – In 1959 various SAS units were re-organised into a mini brigade formation. 21 SAS (formerly The Artists Rifles) became a London based TA unit. 22 SAS became a regular unit based in Hereford and 23 SAS (TA) covered the individual TA squadrons based in the Midlands and the North.

Looking back, fifty years after completing two years full time service, many of the experiences I went through are still fresh in my mind. The culture shock of coming from a comfortable middle-class home where the "F" word and indeed four letter words generally were unknown into a macho Service environment where endless square bashing and pointless "bulling" were the basis of training, and a regime more akin to a prison than to a barracks was the rule, also had a permanent effect.

The disadvantages of National Service included the uncertainty it placed on my subsequent academic and business career. I felt restless after coming out of the army, leaving ICI Witton after six months. I had lost interest in a university course and sought only to make a career in business in an effort to make up what I perceived as lost time. My efforts were rewarded when I eventually qualified first as an accountant then as a company secretary, earning the Institute's Grundy Medal for obtaining highest aggregate marks in the final company secretarial examinations. All the studies for such exams were by way of extramural evening classes and correspondence courses rather than by full time college or university tuition.

The advantages of National Service in my particular case, however, were substantial. I had carried out basic training in a well ordered infantry regiment where accommodation and instructors were better than most. I had had an interesting military career in an overseas posting. I had made many friends, military and civilian, along the way. I had learned much more of other lifestyles, improved my swimming, learned to drive, learned something of man management, learned a little Italian and Arabic, found out far more about classical music, broadcast on the radio, and travelled extensively in the UK, Malta, Tunisia and Libya. A final major benefit was the deep interest in books engendered, which has stayed with me and eventually led to the establishment of my own publishing and printing businesses.

On balance, I benefited from National Service and the experience gave me a respect and affection for the Services which has remained with me through the years. Talking to other ex-National Servicemen, there is a common *esprit de corps*. Although we all remember the rigours of the basic training we endured, the discomfort, occasional boredom and effective loss of liberty for two years we all suffered was balanced by an ability to deal with unforeseen problems, the comradeship we enjoyed with people from all walks of life and the development of an ability to adapt and survive. Not a bad preparation for life.

ABBREVIATIONS

AB64	Army Book 64 (Identity)
ABIII	Army Book III (Discharge)
AEC	Army Education Centre
AECBD	Army Education Central Book Depot
AFRS	American Forces Radio Station
AKC	Army Kinema Corporation
APM	Assistant Provost Marshall
AWOL	Absent Without Leave
BAOR	British Army of the Rhine
BD	Battledress
BMH	British Military Hospital
BOAC	British Overseas Airways Corporation
BRS	British Road Services
BSM	Battery Sergeant Major
CC	Cycling Club
CMD	Command
CO	Commanding Officer
CSM	Company Sergeant Major
DADALS	Deputy Assistant Director, Army Legal Services
DC3	Douglas "Dakota" plane
ERE	Extra Regimentally Employed
FBS	Forces Broadcasting Station
FSMO	Field Service Marching Order
FSS	Field Security Section
HAA	Heavy Anti-Aircraft
HQ	Headquarters
I-Corps	Intelligence Corps
ICI	Imperial Chemical Industries
ID	Identity Document
JTC	Junior Training Corps
KD	Khaki Drill
KES	King Edward's School
LAA	Light Anti-Aircraft
LAD	Light Aid Detachment
LATAS	Libyan American Technical Assistance Service
LMG	Light Machine Gun
LMS	London Midland and Scottish Railway
MCE	Military Corrective Establishment
MI8	Military Intelligence 8
MI9	Military Intelligence 9
MO	Medical Officer

MPSC	Military Provost Staff Corps
MT	Motor Transport
NAAFI	Navy Army and Airforce Institute
NCO	Non-Commissioned Officer
O Level	Ordinary Level
OP	Observation Point
OR	Other Ranks
POW	Prisoner of War
PSO	Personnel Selection Officer
PTI	Physical Training Instructor
PU	Personal Utility
QARANC	Queen Alexandra's Royal Army Nursing Corps
QL	Model Name of Bedford 3 ton Truck
RA	Royal Artillery
RAEC	Royal Army Educational Corps
RAF	Royal Air Force
RAMC	Royal Army Medical Corps
RASC	Royal Army Service Corps
RE	Royal Engineers
REME	Royal Electrical and Mechanical Engineers
RMP	Royal Military Police
RP	Regimental Police
RQMS	Regimental Quarter Master Sergeant
RSM	Regimental Sergeant Major
RTO	Railway Transport Office
RTU	Returned to Unit
RV	Rendezvous
SAC	Strategic Air Command
SAS	Special Air Service
SIB	Special Investigation Branch
SO2	Staff Officer Two
TA	Territorial Army
TCV	Troop Carrying Vehicle
UK	United Kingdom
UN	United Nations
USA	United States of America
VC	Victoria Cross
VIP	Very Important Person
WO	Warrant Officer
WOSB	War Office Selection Board
WW II	The Second World War
YC	Young Conservatives